A True Professional

6 UNIVERSAL AND TIMELESS QUALITIES
30 SPECIFIC BEHAVIORS

Michael O'Donnell

Foreword by
Durward W. Owen

Startupbiz.com, LLC
610 W. Las Olas Blvd, Number 1613
Fort Lauderdale, Florida 33312
http://atruepro.com
E: permissions@atruepro.com

Book Layout ©2017 BookDesignTemplates.com
Cover Image, ©123rf.com/profile_gmast3r

Volume Ordering Information:
Quantity sales and special discounts are available on volume purchases by corporations, non-profits, associations, and others. For details, contact the Special Sales Department: orders@atruepro.com.

A True Professional/ Michael O'Donnell. —1st ed.
ISBN-13: 978-1540849380

CONTENTS

Dedicated to Durward Owen, a maker of true professionals...

...and to my three children, Tyson, Shealee, and Ashton. This book picks up where your mother and I left off.

"A profession is a personal thing that a man acquires. It cannot be inherited. It cannot be bequeathed. Only he, having made the acquisition, puts to use that knowledge and skill with all his ability and complete dedication of purpose can be truly called a professional."

—R.E. ONSTAD

FOREWORD

I am willing to bet that when you left home for the first time to attend college, take a job, or join the military, your parents did not tell you what to do. They simply said, "BE GOOD". This is what my parents said to me and it is what my wife and I said to our children when they left home. It is universal and timeless advice. It is simple, and it is fully understood and appreciated by those whom it is imparted. It does not need to be explained. Such is the advice offered in this book.

None of the qualities or underlining behaviors shared in this book are secrets or revelations; you will recognize most of them. They do not require detailed explanations. Their beauty is their universal truth and simplicity. It is the way in which the author has assembled and condensed them into easily digestible pieces of timeless wisdom which make this book an indispensable blueprint for career success. Indeed; I would argue these qualities and behaviors are not limited to career success. They are immutable guideposts for life success.

Qualities are qualities by any other name, but do you know which specific habits and behaviors determine whether you are endowed with a quality? Which ones are most important for professional development and career advancement? How do you know if others recognize them in you when you have acquired them? These questions are answered in this book.

O'Donnell also offers practical, contemporary strategies and tips for both acquiring the qualities and practicing the behaviors. The vignettes drawn from his personal and professional experiences reinforce their value. His examples are vivid and real, not mere platitudes, because they show how entire careers are made or ruined. In all these ways O'Donnell has advanced the reader's understanding of what it means to be a true professional.

The subject of professionalism has been a big part of my life's work. Allow me to briefly take you back to when it all started for me. In 1964 I was just beginning my career and I made two life changing observations:

First, I was meeting and working with some very successful people. Most of them at the time were fraternity men. Among others, they included Presidents of colleges and universities, industrial companies, financial centers and banks. They were U.S. Senators and Representatives, Governors, military generals and Admirals, railroad presidents, lawyers, doctors, and other highly-regarded leaders. They had all reached the top of their professions.

Secondly, they all shared great commonality in their personal and professional lives. Almost universal were their traits that I had a "checklist" which I followed in evaluating their commonality! My intent was to "be like" these people to the extent possible and just perhaps, I too would be successful. Others must determine if I succeeded or failed; however, others, like you, may want to consider the possibility these observations can help you become more successful than you might otherwise become.

When I accepted the job as Executive Director of a national leadership and educational non-profit, the organization had 52 chapters and 18,925 members. When I retired, the organization had 141 chapters and 69,624 members. The assets of the organization grew 3,000%. Much of this growth and success I attribute to recruiting a top-notch staff, attracting an exceptional board and volunteers at all levels of the organization, and grooming future professionals to one day accept the mantle of leadership.

Over the course of my career I hired and supervised more than 200 staff, most of them recent college graduates who needed to become professionals quickly, if the organization was to achieve its mission. Thus, I taught them the professional qualities and behaviors I observed in successful people -- and that I, myself, tried to practice each day. I led countless workshops for our members and volunteers on the benefits of professionalism. Tens of thousands of people have been exposed to these teachings. Many of them went on to have very successful careers.

The author, Michael O'Donnell, is one of those professionals. I am proud to call him a protégé. I was delighted that he wanted to build on my work and teachings. He took to heart the lessons. He acquired the qualities. He practiced the behaviors. He started with very little in life and worked every day to better himself. He rose to the top of his profession and made meaningful contributions to his community.

Mike has taken these simple, essential behaviors, and made them accessible to all, regardless of profession, without being preachy or judgmental. Through a stream of consciousness, a continuity of subject, and with down-to-earth examples to follow, he guides the reader through both practical and emotional maps which light the path to success in life. He is an able storyteller and standard-bearer for the professional principles I lived by and believe in so passionately. He has lived both successes and failures. He has taken all the world has challenged him with, or attempted to discourage and distract him with, and emerged a true professional. He has perhaps learned the most important lesson of what it means to be a true professional: there are no shortcuts.

So, Mike and I and all the successful people I studied and taught can be your mentors if you so choose. The qualities and behaviors that made us who we are, are all embodied within these pages. It is up to you to act on them. The teachings herein represent a series of simple, small acts, that add up to big results. Mother Teresa said, "There are no great acts, only small acts of great love." To paraphrase that sentiment, there are no great behaviors, only simple behaviors of great professionals, practiced consistently.

You may be wondering, do these qualities and behaviors apply to my generation? Do they speak to my future? Are they relevant today, or will they be relevant in the years to come? Do the internet, mobile devices or online virtual relationships negate the need or importance for any of the qualities and the underlining behaviors championed in this book? I would argue the answer is no. If anything, they are more important than ever because no one can hide any more or cover up their bad behaviors. Everything about one is easily discovered. A professional reputation is more important than ever before.

As the title of this book promises, there are certain qualities and behaviors which are universal and timeless. They determine whether others will hire, promote, invest in and associate with you. They will be just as relevant 100 years from now as they are today and as they were 100 years ago. Learn them. Embody them. Practice them. And then hand them down to the next generation.

To your success and prosperity,

Durward W. Owen
Certified Association Executive (retired)

PREFACE

This book has been 53 years in the making. It spans three generations. It is based partly on the writings and teachings of Durward W. Owen, my first boss and mentor. He wrote the Foreword and his biography is included in the back of this book. I learned the qualities and behaviors of a true professional from him. He taught them to thousands of college students. He practiced them himself and perfected them over many years. He insisted every person who work for him do the same. He always said, "It's just as easy to form good habits as it is to form bad habits."

Durward developed the first set of professional qualities based upon his observations of successful people. Over the course of his esteemed career, he crafted them as a series of anecdotes and gave talks on professionalism all around the country. He swore by these qualities. In some respects, they became the guiding principles of his life.

After learning the qualities from Durward, I practiced them in my career over a 35-year period. I am living proof of how well they work. I know hundreds of amazingly successful people who also learned these qualities from Durward and practiced them to advance their careers. They also swear by them and stand as living testaments to their veracity.

In the Foreword, Durward wrote, "Others must determine how well I succeeded." I can unequivocally testify that he succeeded well beyond his expectations. He taught an entire generation of young people how to become professionals. Many of those to whom he imparted his teachings also succeeded well beyond their own expectations. I am fortunate to be one of those people.

I digested these qualities as if they were a secret formula. They gave me confidence and superhuman strength. When I left the employ of others to start my own company, these qualities and behaviors guided me to success. They helped me to attract investors, hire the best people, and win over customers. They can do the same for you whether you work for an organization or work for yourself. It's now my duty to pass them along to you, the next generation of aspiring professionals.

It is with humility and gratitude that I dedicate this book to Durward W. Owen and thank him for helping all of us to become better versions of ourselves.

Mike O'D

Michael O'Donnell
Entrepreneur/CEO/Author

ACKNOWLEDGEMENTS

Frank MacDonald, Editor
My brother and an accomplished professional in his own right. After a long and distinguished career in telecommunications, Frank now writes science fiction novels and edits them for other sci-fi writers. This was the first non-fiction book he has edited. Good job!

Anthony Phills, Designer
A world-class designer and author of *Designing for the Homerun King*, an illustrated book about his experience designing for the great Baseball player, Barry Bonds. Anthony is the true example for Behavior #23. He designed the cover and other collateral.

Patricia Notarianni, Muse
My better half and inspiration on many levels. She provided the support and encouragement I needed to start and finish this book. Patty is the true example for Behavior #28.

And to my friends and colleagues who reviewed the first draft and offered feedback and suggestions. You continually inspire me to be a better professional and a worthy colleague.

THANK YOU!

DISCLAIMER

INTRODUCTION

L et me just put it out there from the outset, those who knew me when I first started my career would say I am the least likely person they would have expected to write a book on professionalism. I had none of the qualities, I practiced few of the behaviors. I didn't have a clue what it *really* meant to be a professional. Heck, being an entrepreneur isn't even considered to be a profession by most people.

Professionalism wasn't something they taught in school. It wasn't something my parents knew or would have thought to instill. I learned it "on the fly" after entering the workplace, through good role models and bad role models. I was fortunate enough to have a good mentor who helped me to understand the difference. You might not have a good mentor, so honor me with this opportunity to be your guide.

Allow me to first lay the groundwork for what you will find in this book. It may come across a bit academic at first, but stay with me, this isn't a text book. I promise it will get better. Let's get started.

One of the behaviors of a professional is asking a lot of questions. So let's start with the most important ones:

- ➤ <u>Why</u> do you want to be a professional?
- ➤ <u>What</u> does it mean to be a professional?
- ➤ <u>Who</u> can become a professional?
- ➤ <u>How</u> long will it take and how do you do it?
- ➤ Perhaps not as important, but a nagging concern, is the question of whether becoming a professional is a requirement for career success?

Why do you want to be a professional?

Having the reputation as a true professional you will always be in demand. It's as simple as that. You can choose your jobs or clients. You will have all the work you need or want. You will make a good living.

You will be among the few whom others consider indispensable. You will be the "go to" person others rely upon. As a true professional, you will not only be popular with others, you will develop a high sense of purpose and self-worth. You will live a happy and productive life – one worth living.

What does it mean to be a professional?

The term "professional" is bantered around a lot, in numerous forms and in many sectors of society. The dictionary defines a professional as one engaged in a specified activity as one's main paid occupation, rather than as a pastime. The word is often associated with "white collar" workers. It's also a moniker bestowed on those who belong to a "professional" trade association.

The root of professional is "profess", used originally in a religious context to profess an oath to a certain doctrine. Later, it was used in an academic context to describe a "professor", one who had attained the highest academic rank at a university. In the modern era, it is often used to describe athletes who "go pro". These days, it's common to hear every wannabe and wise guy to claim the accolade, as in, "Hey, don't worry about it, I'm a pro!"

Pro is also the root of *progress*, *promote* and *protect*. It's a good way of remembering the benefits of being considered a professional. Being a pro enables you to move forward, move up, and defend your reputation.

Whatever the context, people in all sectors of life recognize the significance of being a professional. But what does it really mean to be one in the eyes of others, especially in the eyes of those who must decide whether to employ you, promote you, invest in you, or associate with you? My first boss, Durward Owen (the inspiration for this book), had a very approachable, egalitarian definition: *A professional is one who goes beyond what is expected of others.*

This is a good definition for approaching this book. You should believe it is a title you can attain. You may already have a reputation as one who goes above and beyond, but do you consistently exceed expectations in all parts and phases of your life? What's the difference between a professional and a *true professional*? If *true* is the qualifier which enables you to stand out from everyone else who claims the title, how do those you work for and associate with discern what is *true*? This book answers these questions by helping you see yourself as others will see you (and talk about you).

Make no mistake, becoming a true professional is not about trying to become a perfect human being. Everyone has flaws. Everyone makes mistakes. No one can be "on" all the time. Being a true professional is about developing certain *qualities* and exhibiting a particular set of *behaviors* most of the time. It is about consistently striving to be the best at what you do for a living. It is about methodically building your reputation and advancing your goals by possessing the "commonality of qualities" as first observed by Durward and later confirmed by thousands of respected professionals who reached the top of their respective professions.

Who can become a professional?

Being a professional is something anyone can be, regardless of his or her line of work, education or training. Professionals are not defined by what they do for a living, but *how* they do it. It is about their behaviors and how they conduct themselves. More importantly, it is a designation which is independently acknowledged by others. It transcends rank and privilege and every other advantage some people may initially have over you. No matter what your natural gifts or inherent limitations, you must earn the right to be called a true professional.

Being a "Professional" is a recognition which you earn every day by exhibiting certain behaviors, and these behaviors are readily observed by others, specifically: those who hire you. A number of these behaviors add up to endow you with certain qualities. Most executives and investors don't consciously think about each and every behavior, but they do recognize the general qualities they collectively represent. They instinctively know them when they see them. They recognize you as having the commonality of qualities they value and respect. They think to themselves, "Now there goes a true professional."

Conversely, whenever a respected decision maker hears another respected decision maker say, "I had an experience with that guy and I found him to be very unprofessional." their ears perk up. They will remember that for a long time. Being called *unprofessional* is one of the worst stains on one's reputation. The reason someone gets tagged with being unprofessional is because they were perceived as missing one or more of the qualities covered in this book. They failed to exhibit one or more of the underlining behaviors.

This book was written to help you learn each quality and each quality's underlining behaviors so that you can internalize them, adapt them, and apply them to ensure your success.

How long will it take you to become a professional and how do you do it?

As a true professional, you will always be a work-in-progress. You will consistently exhibit the qualities and underlying behaviors which are practiced by accomplished people. These behaviors are not things for you to memorize, but things to be and things to do until they become second nature. These behaviors can be adapted by anyone, anywhere, and anytime, but for them to become part of your character they can take years to master.

It's fair to say no one practices all the behaviors...and few of them all the time, but the most successful people will confirm that what they have achieved in life was largely the result of practicing most of these behaviors most of the time. They can recognize these behaviors when they see them in others. If they see them in you, be assured you will become one of the professionals they hire, promote, invest in, and choose to associate with. You will be one of the pros they recommend to their friends, clients and colleagues.

Is becoming a professional a requirement for success?

You may be wondering if becoming a professional is required to be successful. It depends upon how you define success, but generally the answer is no. Some people inherit success. Others just get lucky. All successful people are not professionals, but all true professionals are successful.

Since everyone has their own notion of what it means to be successful, I use the term "accomplished people" in this book to define true professionals. An accomplished person is one recognized and respected by one's peers for consistently conducting oneself professionally and accomplishing meaningful things in one's career. These people achieved these things in their own right, from their own initiatives and dedication. They didn't inherit them or get lucky. Becoming a true professional ensures you will become an accomplished person. Success will follow naturally, no matter how you define it. Albert Einstein perhaps said it best, "Try not to be a person of success, but a person of value."

A word about the six qualities

A quality is a distinctive attribute or characteristic possessed by someone. It is a generally-accepted standard that can be measured against other things of a similar kind. It is the degree of excellence of something. The qualities set forth herein represent the ones observed and documented by Durward when he started studying successful people in the 1960s. These are also the qualities he looked for and developed in the people he hired.

When Durward and I first started collaborating on this subject 25 years ago, we surveyed more than 200 people at the top of their professions. The results confirmed these qualities were the most valued by these accomplished people. These qualities both propelled these professionals to the top and are the ones they most valued in those they hired and chose to associate with. Over the years I have read countless books and articles on the qualities of accomplished people. Without fail, the six qualities presented in this book represent the "commonality of qualities" most often attributed to accomplished people.

A word about the 30 behaviors

Durward believed the DNA of each quality was comprised of certain "traits". He was quick to say, however, these are learned traits. One is not born with them. To avoid the nature vs. nurture debate, I have chosen to characterize the DNA of qualities as "behaviors" instead of traits. If it suits you to think of them as traits or habits, more power to you. Just know that anyone can learn, practice and apply them.

You must believe you are fully capable of acquiring these behaviors, internalizing them and adapting them to become a true pro, as duly recognized by others. For example, you were not born with manners, or with the ability to speak multiple languages, correct? These are learned behaviors. And so it is with the behaviors to become a true professional. They can be learned and customized to compliment your unique character and personality. Most importantly, they can be practiced and applied to advance your career and professional stature.

Regarding the number of behaviors, there is no magic to the number 30. In this book, there are five behaviors that comprise each quality. They are designed to describe what it means to have each of the qualities. We can debate their descriptions. We can argue for a shorter or longer list, but to do so would either do one or more behaviors an injustice by exclusion, or make the list so long it would comprise the entirety of human personality with little attention to the true meaning of professionalism.

You might be wondering, "Do I have to exhibit all five behaviors to be recognized as having the quality?" In my experience, the answer is no, practicing just two or three of them can distinguish you from most other aspiring professionals. Of course, the more of the behaviors you practice, the easier it is for employers, clients, investors, leaders, and your peers and associates, to conclude without a doubt, that you are a true pro.

The one thing you should not do is confuse these behaviors with clichés and platitudes. Some people will look at the list and quickly dismiss it has obvious or dated. Some will say to themselves, "yeah, we all know that" but they will fail to truly understand what each behavior means and the integral role each plays in developing a quality and how it contributes to one becoming an accomplished person. Each behavior is universal and timeless because it can be practiced by anyone and has no expiration date.

Book format

This book is divided into six chapters. Each chapter represents one of the key qualities possessed by true professionals. True professionals are **Groomed, Knowledgeable, Connected, Aware, Timely,** and **Polished.**

Each quality is comprised of <u>five</u> specific behaviors that endow a true professional with the quality. It is not enough to simply say one is "groomed". We must understand what it means to be groomed. Note that each behavior begins with a verb, because they are things to do and be, not just things to learn.

Each behavior is introduced by a *quote* from an accomplished person. The quote encapsulates the core message of the behavior. Next is an *explanation* of what it means to exhibit the behavior. You may not see yourself in each of these explanations yet, but one day you will.

The explanation is followed by a *true example* of one who succeeded because they exhibited the behavior, or failed because they did not. Many of the examples are true stories from my personal journey to become a true professional.

The example is followed by a *data point* which visually supports the importance of the behavior. The behavior is not just my opinion, its validity is supported by independent research and fact. The data point is followed by *strategies and tips* for acquiring and applying the behavior.

The strategies and tips are followed by *the final word* inspired by someone who is widely known for personifying the behavior. Finally, each behavior concludes with a list of *Good reads and resources* for additional edification. *Interactive resources* are also available online at *http://atruepro.com*.

The qualities and behaviors do not appear in any order of priority. You can start anywhere in the book you like. Start with **Polished** and work your way forward to **Groomed** if it suits you. Being **Knowledgeable** is no more or no less important than being **Aware**. You don't have to be **Connected** before you can become **Timely**. It is the totality of the behaviors you possess of each quality that is important. You will likely find you already possess a good number of them, and that some are more difficult to practice than others. Each behavior is meant to be continually refined and perfected throughout your entire professional career.

All-in-all, this book offers 6 qualities, 30 behaviors, 30 inspirational quotes, 30 explanations of what it means to be a true pro, 30 true examples, 30 data points, 240 strategies and tips, 30 final words inspired by true pros, and a long list of resources for professional improvement. Each behavior is worth its weight in gold. Collectively, they are priceless.

Symbols

Some behaviors are meant to be <u>internalized</u> until they become habits and are practiced subconsciously. They are designated with the (IN) symbol. Other behaviors are meant to be <u>adapted</u> to a given personal or professional situation. They are designated with the (AD) symbol.

(IN) = **In**ternalize the behavior until it becomes second nature.

(AD) = **Ad**apt the behavior to situations as appropriate.

You and Me

Finally, most of these pages are written in the first and second person. I want to have a conversation with YOU. This was written for you. I want you to see yourself in these examples. The goal is to know what qualities and underlining behaviors will make you a true professional, and to learn how to apply and practice them, so they help augment and compliment the special human being you already are.

My hope is this book will be a blueprint for your career success. This is the promise I make to you by reading this book, taking to heart its lessons, and assimilating these qualities:

You will transform yourself from an aspiring professional into a true professional, and you will succeed in your profession and in life beyond your wildest expectations. Enjoy the journey!

CHAPTER 1

GROOMED

This is the OUTWARD you, how you appear to others and how you feel <u>physically</u> about yourself.

It's about dress, etiquette, diet and exercise, moderation, and rest.

1. Dress one step above those you are dealing with.

The American costume designer who won a record eight Academy Awards for Best Costume Design, Edith Head, said it best: *"You can have anything you want. If you dress for it."*

Y ou get the idea. How you dress will influence your success! True professionals know they must look the part to get the part. This includes grooming, which is too often overlooked as an important part of one's appearance. Grooming appeals to two of our senses: sight and smell. It's a simple fact of life that people are attracted to people who stimulate these senses and they virtually don't see people who do not. True professionals know it is character that determines human worth, but they realize it is their appearance which others will first judge them by.

What does it mean to dress one step above those you are dealing with?

As a true professional, you dress appropriately for your office culture and important social occasions. You blend in, but you are never overlooked. The people you work with take notice of what you wear, because you are usually sporting a little something extra than most everyone else. You're in style, but your attire is adapted to be uniquely yours. Your "signature look" is an authentic expression of who you are, but it doesn't threaten or offend the sensibilities of those you associate with. You are impeccably groomed. People often comment on how "sharp" you look.

A true example

Allow me to relay a true story about my own professional debut. In 1981 I moved from Florida to North Carolina to go to work for Durward Owen. I arrived with the clothes I wore in Florida as a college student. My wardrobe consisted largely of silk flower shirts and bell bottom jeans. My "work" attire consisted of gaudy leisure suits, where I folded the collars of my flowery silk shirts OVER the collar of the leisure suit jacket. That was the look du jour. For a visual, you can Google leisure suit – truly hideous. To top it off, I had very long hair.

My job was going to be consulting with student leaders and persuading successful businessmen to contribute to a national foundation. Durward took one look at me on my first day of work and said, "That's not going to work." I was a bit offended because I rather liked my long hair, my leisure suits and silk flower shirts, but I realized my look was a tad dated and I knew better than to argue the point with my new boss. Being my first job, I had no money, so Durward gave me his credit card and the name of a store where I could buy some new duds. After getting a haircut, off I went to acquire a new wardrobe.

The next day and $700 lighter, Durward came by my apartment to pick up his credit card and check out my new wardrobe. I proudly threw open the closet doors and said "Voila!" Very proud of my new look was I. Durward burst into laughter.

There, hanging in the closet, were a half dozen flower print shirts – polyester, not silk, mind you. The shirts were matched with polyester slacks, colorful wide ties, and an ill-fitting polyester jacket. I had essentially purchased the same style of clothing because I did not know how to adapt to the appropriate style for the work I would be doing. You can take the surfer boy out of Florida, but you can't take Florida out of the surfer boy, until you give him an entirely new frame of reference.

To remedy the situation, Durward had me read the book "Dress for Success". He then had one of his seasoned employees go with me back to the store to exchange the clothes for all new clothes more appropriate for the work I would be doing. In short order, I was sporting button-down starched cotton shirts, sharply creased khaki's, thin ivy league ties, and shiny penny loafers. The ensemble was topped off with a perfectly fitted blue blazer with beautiful gold buttons. The transformation was complete: I looked like a true professional. My charges and my targets would now take me seriously.

Durward said frequently, "You never get a second chance to make a good first impression." As a policy, he required all his employees who were attending an industry event to show up on the first day in coat and tie, even if the dress for the event was business casual. We always made an initial appearance dressed a step above our peers. During the week, we dressed down a bit, on the same level as everyone else in attendance. On the last day, we departed again in coat and tie. The first thing and the last thing people remembered about us was how well attired we were.

Later in my career I doubled-down on this behavior. As an aspiring entrepreneur, I needed to raise several million dollars to launch a new venture. I was raising three kids, had a mortgage and two car payments. I could ill afford to invest in a new suit, but I had the opportunity to pitch an investment bank in New York. I visited a professional clothier and said, "Make me look like I am deserving of a million bucks." The tab was $1,500. It was by far the most expensive suit I had ever purchased, but it made me look like a million bucks and, more importantly, it made me feel like a million bucks. I got the money and my company was successfully launched.

Data point

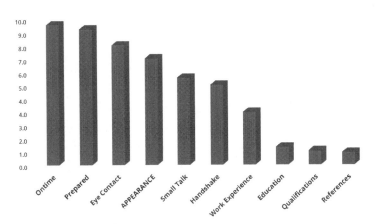

Source: Monster.uk.com

According to a survey of 273 hiring managers, appearance is more important than work experience, education, qualifications and references in the first interview. Appearance, eye contact, and handshake create the first impression. Hiring managers say they know within six minutes of starting the interview whether a job candidate will be seriously considered.

Strategies and tips for dressing one step above those you are dealing with

 So how do you put this adaptive behavior into practice?

First, be aware of the dress culture of the people you will be dealing with, then choose a look that is compatible with the culture, but adds your own unique spin. For example, one high tech executive I knew always wore a beautiful suit, but with RED sneakers. It sounds weird, but he pulled it off and it made him look like a stylish, if not somewhat eccentric genius. There was a period in my career where all men wore a suit in the workplace. I wore mine with pleated pants, cuffs, a bowtie and suspenders. My ensemble made me standout and elicited a steady stream of compliments from my associates.

Second, focus on good fit. The way your clothes fit can make or break your entire appearance. Clothing too tight fitting can make you look frumpy. Clothing too baggy can make you look disheveled. Your clothes should also fit your body style. Men should take care to ensure their ties and slacks are not too short unless you are going for a dorky look. Women should take care to ensure their skirts are not too short and their blouses too tight. That's not the kind of attention you want. You want to be attractive, but not too suggestive, unless it's in an appropriate social setting. A good clothier can help you with the proper fit.

Third, be consistent. Dressing consistently communicates reliability. Think of your professional attire as a uniform. It should create an aura of uniformity about you. Uniformity demonstrates commitment and builds trust among your associates. In the true example above, my first uniform consisted of button-down shirt, kaki's, ivy league tie, blue blazer and penny loafers. Although the color of my shirt and tie varied day-to-day, the overall look was consistent and uniform.

Fourth, be coordinated, purchase pieces of your attire to mix-and-match. A coordinated outfit subconsciously projects to others that you are organized and efficient. Since you probably can't afford to wear an entirely new outfit every day, choose shirts or blouses which can be worn with a variety of different slacks and blazers. Choose ties or scarves that will match every outfit.

Fifth, keep it simple. You are an animate object in constant motion. You need to sit, stand, walk, and sometimes run. If your attire restricts your motion you'll look and feel awkward, and be downright miserable. Don't over accessorize, or over complicate your wardrobe. As you will see later, time is a weapon and another important behavior of true professionals. If it takes you too long to get ready or to move, you will be putting yourself at a disadvantage. You can always tell a person who has over dressed. He or she is always fidgeting, pulling on this, pushing on that, fighting with their clothes as if they were an invading enemy.

Sixth, your dress is only as good as your overall grooming. How you are groomed will either destroy whatever look you are striving for, or it will accentuate it perfectly. Men, please trim those wild eyebrows and the hair growing out of your nose and ears. It's not a good look. Women, your colleagues will love your manicured nails, but they don't have to be long and sharp as knives, nor works of art. And please don't overdo the perfume!

Seventh, a good hair cut is priceless. It is one of the things people notice first about you and will likely be the thing they will comment on the most. How many times have you heard, "Nice haircut" or "I love what you've done to your hair!".

Finally, double check for body odor and bad breath. It won't matter how nicely you are dressed if your very presence is pungent or offensive to others. Hopefully your spouse, roommate or dear friends will love you enough to clue you in if something smells amiss. If not, you can usually catch a hint from the way people react to you: they will politely keep their distance.

The Final Word, by Daymond John[1]

"Good grooming is integral and impeccable style is a must. If you don't look the part, no one will want to give you time or money."

Good reads and resources

John T. Molloy's New Dress for Success
by John T. Molloy

New Women's Dress for Success
by John T. Molloy

The Truth About Style
by Stacy London

Dressing the Man: Mastering the Art of Permanent Fashion
by Alan Flusser

How to Get Dressed: A Costume Designer's Secrets for Making Your Clothes
Look, Fit, and Feel Amazing
by Alison Freer

AskMen.com Presents The Style Bible: The 11 Rules for Building a Complete
and Timeless Wardrobe by James Bassil

Everyday Icon: Michelle Obama and the Power of Style
by Kate Betts

Man Up!: 367 Classic Skills for the Modern Guy
by Paul O'Donnell

2. Dine using proper etiquette for the occasion.

One of the foremost authorities on etiquette is the incomparable Judith Martin, a.k.a. Miss Manners. She summed it up this way: *"You can deny all you want that there is etiquette, and a lot of people do in everyday life. But if you behave in a way that offends the people you're trying to deal with, they will stop dealing with you...Etiquette doesn't have the great sanctions that the law has. But the main sanction we do have is in not dealing with these people and isolating them because their behavior is unbearable."*

Good etiquette, of course, encompasses a wide range of social norms. We will touch on some additional ones in other sections of this book. Good table manners are perhaps the foundation for all proper etiquette, because "breaking bread" with someone is a centuries old ritual which can forge a profitable new relationship, or forever extinguish it from taking hold. If you have ever dined with someone who did not know how to handle a knife and fork, talked with their mouth full, or discussed things which made you lose your appetite, then you know dining etiquette is an important behavior which strongly influences how you are perceived by others.

How you conduct yourself during meals, specifically in a business setting, speaks volumes about you. When you eat with the hiring team during a job interview, they are not concerned about how hungry you are, or if your meal is satisfying. They are consciously or subconsciously observing your habits and manners. Good manners are not always acknowledged, but bad manners are always noticed. How you eat at home or in the company of family and close friends is of lesser importance. Adapting how you eat and drink in the company of associates to conform to proper etiquette is a behavior of a true professional. Heed the words of Mark Twain: "Laws control the lesser man. Right conduct controls the greater."

What does it mean to dine using proper etiquette for the occasion?

As a true professional, you observe and practice the decorum which is appropriate for the occasion. At a dinner party, you wait for the host to motion towards the seat you are to take, and wait for the host to be seated before seating yourself. Approaching any table alongside other guests, you take your chair from the left-hand side and exit on the right. In most settings, you wait for everyone at the table to be served before beginning to eat. In a formal setting, you wait for the host to start first.

You know how to use the silverware and which order to use it (the outside in). The number of silverware pieces tells you how many courses to expect, so you can pace yourself accordingly. Your napkin is placed in your lap after your host takes hers from the table. You know how to give and participate in a toast before the meal begins. You know the proper way to eat certain foods, especially which are finger foods and which require use of the silverware. You know how to pass dishes across the table. You always pass the salt and pepper together (to the right), even if the person requested only one of them. You eat at the same pace as most people at the table, taking your cues from the host.

A True Example

While on a roadshow in New York City to raise capital for my company, I was invited to have dinner with an investment banker who also happened to serve on the city council. He told me to meet him at the 21 Club in Manhattan at 6pm sharp. I mentioned my dinner plans to another investor I was meeting with earlier in the day. He was impressed by who I was meeting with and where we were dining. He said, "If you want to make an impression, order the Steak Tartare. It's not on the menu, but it's an old favorite going back to the days when the place was a speakeasy in 1929. Only locals know about the dish and the chef will make it upon special request."

At 6pm sharp I eagerly entered the club. I had not eaten all day because of back-to-back meetings. I was starving. As I approached the reception stand the maître d looked horrified. He barked, "Young man, come with me!" He ushered me into a backroom where he promptly admonished me for not wearing a tie. He explained that if it were not for the fact I was there to meet the councilmen, he would be obliged to ask me to leave. He opened a drawer to expose a row of ties and asked me to select one. Now properly attired, I was escorted into the lounge where the councilmen awaited.

After apologizing for being late and improperly attired, we ordered drinks. The councilmen ordered a Scotch, neat. I asked the waiter what types of beers they had. He recoiled and then replied, "I'm not quite sure, I will need to check." The councilmen raised his eyebrows and winced. "On second thought," I said quickly, "I will have what the councilmen is drinking."

Three hours and several drinks later, we were still sitting in the lounge talking about my business. I thought I was going to pass out from hunger as I was peppered with questions and pressed for details. Top that off with the fact I was not a scotch drinker, but trying to match my host drink-for-drink. No doubt I was not as articulate as I should have been making the case for why my company would be a good investment. Finally, the waiter came over to announce that our table was ready.

We entered the main dining room which was packed with important people and buzzing with loud conversation. Unbeknownst to me, it's customary for a politician to make a grand entrance and then saunter slowly through the room, stopping to say hello to the luminaries and donors at every table on the way to his own table. At this point, I was about to faint. I was inebriated, a bit disheveled, and probably looked like I was going to be sick. My opportunity to make a good impression, and to make my host look good, had long past.

We finally made it to our table and ordered. As the host, the councilmen beckoned me to go first. This was the moment to redeem myself. I pulled myself together and confidently looked up to the waiter. "I'd like to have the Steak Tartare please." The waiter looked surprised. "Very GOOD sir," he replied. The councilmen smiled and nodded his approval. He then ordered a ribeye with baked potato. I was salivating.

Now this is the point in the story where I must confess I had no idea what Steak Tartare was. I wasn't that worldly of a guy at that stage in my career and had little culinary experience. Hey, it had the word "steak" in it so that sounded good to me. The dish arrived on a platter covered with a large silver cover. The waiter made a great show of slowly placing the platter in front of me, then quickly removing the cover. Voila!

There it was. A huge plate of raw hamburger with an equally raw egg on top. For a minute, I thought the councilmen was pulling a joke on me. I began to laugh. The waiter looked concerned. "Is it not to your liking, sir?" he asked. The councilmen stared at me with furrowed brow. Realizing it was no joke, I starred at it as if it would be my last meal and muttered, "It looks amazing." I did my best to eat it, but the hunger, the drinks and the stress, got the better of me. I excused myself from the table and fled to the bathroom, where I upchucked what little contents was in my stomach.

Suffice it to say I did not get the investment, but I learned an important lesson. Dining etiquette is not just about table manners. It is also knowing the proper attire and understanding the social norms and customs of those whom you are dining with. It's knowing a little something about the dishes you will be served, and pacing yourself appropriately through the entire event. Dining etiquette is not about eating, but the entire experience and pageantry of dining with others in a formal (or professional) setting.

Data point

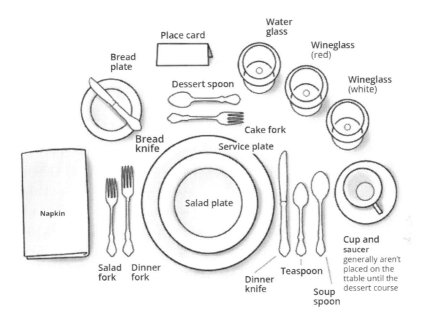

Source: Emily Post Institute

The table place setting arrangement varies across cultures and by type of occasion. The formal place setting depicted here is common in American culture. The placement of utensils is guided by the menu, the idea being that you use utensils in an "outside in" order.

Strategies and tips for dining using proper etiquette for the occasion

 So how do you put this adaptive behavior into practice?

First, understand the meal is not about YOU (unless you are the host). Only an inconsiderate, unprofessional social dolt would take a call or text during a meal with clients. Only a clueless, self-absorbed unprofessional would dominate the conversation or make it all about them, even if dining with associates instead of clients. Silence your devices and be prepared to engage in conversation with your host and other people at the table.

Second, if you need to step away from the table to take an important call or use the restroom, don't announce your intentions. Simply say, 'excuse me,' and step away. Never take a call at the table! When returning to the table, only apologize if you have been away for an inordinate amount of time. Say something like, 'What did I miss?' Signal to those at the table that you are reengaging; focusing again on them and the conversation at hand, and not otherwise preoccupied with whatever it was that took you away from the table.

Third, be sensitive to the decorum expected for the occasion and by those with whom you are dining. Unless it is customary, and until the host takes the lead, do not smoke or order an alcoholic beverage. No matter how relaxed the atmosphere, try to keep your elbows off the table and, for heaven's sake, don't talk with your mouth full!

Fourth, if you must cough, sneeze or belch, turn your head and do it as discreetly as possible into your left hand (unless you are left-handed), with a handkerchief (always carry one when dining with others). You shake with your right hand, no one at the table wants to picture themselves having to shake hands with you after you coughed into it, or wiped your nose with it.

Fifth, avoid bringing up sensitive issues until you know where everyone stands. There's a good rule to remember in social situations: never hold an election until you have first counted the votes. It's common to discuss politics and religion, and to respectfully disagree with the opinions of others, but do so in a thoughtful manner. There should be no right or wrong, no black or white in your tone, but an open and receptive exchange of diverse opinions. Try to avoid using off-color language and making sweeping generalizations like, `All liberals are fiscally irresponsible,' or 'All conservatives are greedy capitalists.'

Sixth, don't make your dietary restrictions everyone else's problem. If ordering in a restaurant, speak your restrictions quietly to the waiter, don't dramatize them. If attending a dinner party at someone's home or office, speak to the host ahead of time so he or she is not embarrassed by serving you something you cannot eat. If you are brought dessert without ordering it, don't refuse it. Gracefully accept it, compliment it, then politely offer it to someone else at the table.

Seventh, when acknowledging someone at the table or someone else in the room seated at another table, never point at them or waive your fork or knife at them. Dining is not a duel. Acknowledge them with an open palm wave. And, of course, never shout across the room or speak too loudly to someone across the table. Keep your voice at the same level as the other conversation at the table.

Finally, pace yourself through the entire meal and mind how you address the wait staff. Your food is not something to be attacked, nor should you be the last to finish the meal. If wine or other alcoholic beverages are being served, drink them at the pace of the others at the table. Nothing is more disconcerting to others than watching someone at the table chug down drinks like he is at a fraternity beach party. Be polite to the wait staff, saying please and thank you. Many a candidate lost the job or promotion because of acting superior or rude to the staff.

The Final Word, by Jacqueline Whitmore[2]

"Whenever we make a mistake such as talking with a mouthful of food, ordering the wrong kinds of foods or holding our fork like a shovel, we ruin a relationship and diminish our personal brand."

Good reads and resources

The Complete Life
by John Erskine

How to Be Socially Savvy in All Situations
by Joy Weaver

Poised for Success,
by Jacqueline Whitmore

Global Etiquette Guide
by Dean Allen

The Forgetful Gentleman
by Nathan Tan

Mind Your Digital Manners: Advice for an Age Without Rules
by Steven Petrow

Modern Manners: Tools to Take You to the Top
by Dorothea Johnson

Would It Kill You to Stop Doing That: A Modern Guide to Manners
by Philip Galanes

How to Be a Gentleman: A Timely Guide to Timeless Manners
by John Bridges

3. Maintain a healthy diet, exercise regularly and stay fit.

The man called the "Godfather of Fitness", Jack LaLanne, nailed it when he said, *"Your health account, your bank account, they're the same thing. The more you put in, the more you can take out. Exercise is king and nutrition is queen. Together you have a kingdom."*

People like to hire, invest in, and associate with people who look fit and capable. To look the part, act the part, and be the part, true professionals take care of themselves. They invest in their health and well-being. They don't just go through the motions; they internalize fitness so it becomes a habit, a behavior, an important part of their character. They don't talk about "getting around to it", they schedule it and live it, as critical and as natural as breathing.

What does it mean to maintain a healthy diet, exercise regularly and stay fit?

As a true professional, you eat balanced meals and you are conscious of good nutrition. You don't make fast food a routine. You watch your weight. You practice portion control, eating what your body needs until it is full, and not until everything on your plate might be gone. You try to manage your sugar intake. You take supplements or protein shakes with vitamins and minerals when you are unable to eat three good meals a day.

You work out or do something active several times a week. You take the stairs instead of the escalator or elevator when possible. You schedule regular time at the gym and rarely miss the appointment, or you join a company or community sports league. You get at least 20 minutes of sustained exercise at least three times per week, within safe physical limits. You are as physically active as your age and general health allows you to be. You try to get a good night's sleep every day.

A true example

After I had started a family and acquired some wealth, I received a call out of the blue from an old college buddy. I was flattered to hear he had been following my career and knew of some of my successes. He said he was a financial planner and was hoping I would give him some time to discuss my investments and estate planning. He was with a well-respected company and I certainly needed some planning assistance at that stage in my life, so I graciously accepted his invitation. We agreed to meet for coffee.

When he walked into the coffee shop, 10 minutes late, I barely recognized him. He was my age, but looked at least 10 years older. He was at least 30 lbs. overweight. He looked jaundiced and his hair was brittle. We exchanged pleasantries, swapped some stories, and then he launched into his presentation. As he talked, he paused occasionally to munch on a muffin and gulp down coffee. During our ensuing conversation, he wheezed and coughed and eventually had to excuse himself to go outside for a smoke.

All I could think about was how handsome and fit he was in college. The girls all adored him and the guys all looked up to him. Now, here he was just 15 years later, a physical wreck. If this guy couldn't take care of himself, why would I trust him to take care of my investments, or help plan my family's future? All the work his company had done to build a reputation over many years and produce expensive client literature was shattered for me in under an hour. I felt sorry for him, but pity is the last thing a true professional wants from his associates.

It may sound unfair, but why would I trust a company that would hire (or keep) a guy who didn't respect himself? Every employee reflects the enterprise he or she works for. It's guilt by association and the hard, cold, cruel facts of life are smart companies don't hire people who don't take care of themselves, and they find ways to get rid of them if they fail to stay fit after they hire them. It's too expensive, and bad for a company's reputation, to employ unhealthy people who choose to be so because of bad lifestyle choices.

Data point

Balanced Diet | Regular Exercise

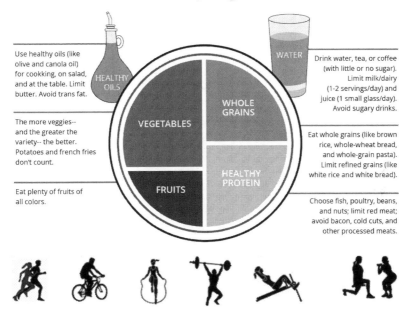

Use healthy oils (like olive and canola oil) for cookking, on salad, and at the table. Limit butter. Avoid trans fat.

The more veggies-- and the greater the variety-- the better. Potatoes and french fries don't count.

Eat plenty of fruits of all colors.

Drink water, tea, or coffee (with little or no sugar). Limit milk/dairy (1-2 servings/day) and juice (1 small glass/day). Avoid sugary drinks.

Eat whole grains (like brown rice, whole-wheat bread, and whole-grain pasta). Limit refined grains (like white rice and white bread).

Choose fish, poultry, beans, and nuts; limit red meat; avoid bacon, cold cuts, and other processed meats.

Source: Harvard School of Public Health

Most experts agree people don't consume enough fruits and vegetables. They should represent half of the meal. The other half should consist of grains and protein. The most important thing is to MINIMIZE the amount of sugar you consume, especially sugar in processed foods. It's a serious health issue.

Strategies and tips for maintaining a healthy diet, exercising regularly and staying fit

 So how do you put this internalized behavior into practice?

First, make nutrition and exercise a priority; a mindset. Schedule them and commit to them. Plan your meals, track your caloric intake. Your health is literally a life and death matter. If you don't manage it properly you will die physically, mentally, emotionally and professionally. Say to yourself every day until it becomes a behavior you don't even have to think about: "Good health is a lifestyle choice, and I choose to be as healthy as I possibly can be."

Second, exercise daily in-place. No matter where you are or what you are doing, take a few minutes to move your body every hour. You can stand, shake, stretch, use dumbbells or do isometric exercises at your desk or watching TV. Get up from your desk several times each day and take a quick walk around the building. Walk to lunch and take the stairs whenever possible. They even make miniature treadmills these days you can slide under your desk.

Third, replace physical activity you dislike with an activity you love. If you hate running, or going to the gym, for crying out loud stop doing it! All you are doing is reinforcing a negative. Turn it into a positive. Perhaps you like to wade in a pool, play tennis, garden, or ride a bike? Do those things and stop beating yourself up for not working out like others do.

Fourth, share desserts and exercise with a partner. No need to give up sweets, just cut back on them. They are a great opportunity to share with others. Find someone to walk with, bike with, swim with, or play a sport with. A friendly competition is both motivating and stimulating. Admit it, you're competitive; otherwise you wouldn't be reading this book. Even if you are only competing against yourself, set goals and milestones to beat. Challenge yourself to be more fit next year than you are this year.

Fifth, hire a nutritionist and/or a trainer. If you need a push or some guidance, there are thousands of people who do this for a living. If you are on a tight budget, barter with them. I once hired a trainer and paid him with in kind services by writing a marketing plan for him.

Sixth, eat a light lunch and try not to eat right before going to bed. Give your body time to burn calories. Eat healthy snacks during the day to ward off hunger and to keep your energy level up. Most importantly, practice portion control. It's not just what you eat, but how much you eat. Eating 5-6 small meals each day is better than eating 3 big meals.

Seventh, take power naps. At my company, we had a nap room. Lots of companies now encourage their employees to take a short nap. A 20-30-minute nap is scientifically proven to improve alertness and performance without leaving you feeling groggy or interfering with nighttime sleep.

Finally, learn to love what you cannot change and proactively manage it. You may be a large person because of genetics. You may suffer from thyroid problems or a chronic health disease. If you can't cure it, manage it. Being a fit professional does not mean you have a perfect body or perfect health – few people do. It means you accept who you are and what health challenges you have inherited, then proactively deal with them head on to minimize any negative impact they have on living a full and productive life.

The Final Word, by Kayla Itsines[3]

> "Some days you eat salads and go to the gym, some days you eat cupcakes and refuse to put on pants. It's called balance."

Good reads and resources

Eat to Live: The Amazing Nutrient-Rich Program for Fast and Sustained Weight Loss
by Joel Fuhrman

The China Study: The Most Comprehensive Study of Nutrition Ever Conducted And the Startling Implications for Diet, Weight Loss, And Long-term Health
by Thomas Campbell

Eat Right for Your Type: Complete Blood Type Encyclopedia
by Peter D'Adamo and Catherine Whitney

ACSM's Guidelines for Exercise Testing and Prescription
by American College of Sports Medicine

Thinner Leaner Stronger: The Simple Science of Building the Ultimate Female Body
by Michael Matthews

100 No-Equipment Workouts Vol. 1: Fitness Routines you can do anywhere, Any Time
by Neila Rey

Fit for Life
by Harvey Diamond and Marilyn Diamond

The 22 Non-Negotiable Laws of Wellness: Take Your Health into Your Own Hands to Feel, Think, and Live Better Than You Ever Thought Possible
by Greg Anderson

The Wellness Workbook, 3rd ed: How to Achieve Enduring Health and Vitality
by John W. Travis and Regina Sara Ryan

4. Avoid excesses and extremes, practice moderation in all things.

The timeless philosopher Aristotle said, *"Moderation in all things is the key to success."* He also said, *"We are what we repeatedly do. Excellence, therefore, is not an act, but a habit."* He died in the year 322 BC and his advice is just as pertinent today.

U.S. Supreme Court Justice Sonia Sotomayor remarked, "My diabetes is such a central part of my life... it did teach me discipline... it also taught me about moderation... I've trained myself to be super-vigilant... because I feel better when I am in control."

The accomplished men and women of history developed early on the discipline to avoid excesses and extremes, and to practice moderation in their personal and professional lives. One of the great writers and philosophers of his time, Voltaire said, "Use, do not abuse... neither abstinence nor excess ever renders man happy."

True professionals know that too much of anything, especially a good thing, is counterproductive to the benefits and enjoyment that come from having the thing in the first place. Very successful people have been known to go on a "bender" from time-to-time, they just don't let it become a habit. They know the practice of moderation leads to the ultimate life experience: the fulfillment of one's potential.

What does it mean to avoid excesses and extremes, and practice moderation in all things?

As a true professional, you don't overindulge in anything when among your work associates or clients. You may stretch a few things from time to time at home among family and friends, but as a practice you maintain a healthy balance in all things. Whether it be work, food, drink, smoke, medications, sex, shopping, cursing, gambling, television, video games, Internet surfing or social media, whatever it is, you know when to STOP, take a break and walk away.

If you have an addictive personality, an obsessive-compulsive disorder, or are otherwise susceptible to overdoing something, you have learned to avoid what triggers it and developed strategies for controlling it. You listen to your internal early warning system to hit the shutoff valve before going too far. When you start sliding a bit, and we all do, you have the strength of character to listen to someone who suggests you should stop, or dial it back. You realize the single biggest reason people self-destruct and ruin their careers is because of excesses and extremes they could not recover from – and you are determined never to become one of those people.

A true example

Success can breed excess, and eventually destroy one's career and marriage. Such is the story of my former neighbor. Chuck was a rising star in a prominent law firm. He was the youngest attorney to ever make partner. He was bright, ambitious, and well-liked by all who knew him. He had a beautiful wife, three wonderful kids, and a big house in the suburbs. He was living the American dream.

Chuck loved to play poker. We had a neighborhood poker game every month; friendly stakes. Chuck won more than he lost. At the end of every game he would joke, "Ya'll can come over my house and visit your money anytime you want." Chuck was a winner.

Unbeknownst to most of us, Chuck also had a gambling problem. What little money he won from his neighbors would be blown along with tens of thousands of dollars at the local casino. He was also known to fly to Las Vegas frequently. Chuck, like many gamblers, thought he could beat the house. Unfortunately, the house always wins in the end.

As Chuck's losses mounted, he began gambling more often and much larger amounts of money to try and recover his losses. This behavior led to the classic vicious cycle which consumes people who fail to recognize their actions and moderate accordingly. What's more, it spilled over into other forms of bad judgment and addictive behaviors. Chuck began having an affair with his secretary at work. She loved trips to Vegas and the gifts he lavished upon her.

There is so much more to this story, most of it painful, but I can stop here. You can see a train wreck when it is coming. You may have guessed it: Chuck lost his job, his wife and his kids. The girlfriend didn't stick around long either. The last time I talked to him he had moved in with his mother and father and was practicing as a sole practitioner. He still makes frequent trips to Las Vegas.

Data point

How Much is Too Much?

Men	Women
More than 2 drinks a day.	More than 1 drinks a day.

Source: Centers for Disease Control and Prevention

Excessive alcohol use, including underage drinking and binge drinking (drinking 5 or more drinks on an occasion for men or 4 or more drinks on an occasion for women), can lead to increased risk of health problems such as injuries, violence, liver diseases, and cancer. One in ten deaths of all working-aged people is caused by excessive alcohol consumption.

Strategies and tips for avoiding excesses and extremes, and practicing moderation in all things

 So how do you put this internalized behavior into practice?

First, make <u>balance</u> a guiding principle of your lifestyle. Moderation is about finding a balance between two extremes: deprivation and overindulging. Avoid the yoyo effect by seeking middle ground. Neither completely deprive yourself of the things you desire, nor revolve your life around them. A healthy routine which provides good balance must be internalized and practiced as habit. If you try to adapt moderation to a given vice or situation, you will forever be swinging between two extremes. Internalize moderation so it becomes second nature.

Second, be on guard against the slippery slope. Say no to regular binges and cheat days, no matter how harmless they may seem. It is easy to rationalize the "weekly" binge or to make Saturdays the day you can overindulge. When you do that, you are programming your brain and your body to embrace extremes. Eventually, that behavior will catch up with you and, before you know it, you will be binging or cheating several days a week.

Third, reward balance and moderation by indulging (but not over-indulging) in the things you enjoy periodically. In fact, you will enjoy your indulgences that much more if they are taken in moderation. You can plan your treats like you plan a vacation. But like a vacation, schedule a reasonable start and end time, and set a budget. For example, if you enjoy gambling, schedule a date to visit a casino and set a limit on the time and amount of money you will spend while there.

Fourth, limit access to or the amount of the thing you want to indulge in. Remove from your home and office all the things that tempt you. If you're a workaholic, set the lights to go off in your office at a certain time. If you want to munch while watching TV, don't sit down with an entire bag of chips, put a handful in a bowl. If you enjoy a cigar occasionally, don't buy an entire case, buy one at a time. Out of sight, out of mind, is a good strategy.

Fifth, listen to how you feel; trust your mind and your instincts. Most people get into trouble because they ignore their own conscience or the signals their bodies are sending their mind. Most people have a self-control meter.

Heed it! If you have faulty wiring and your self-control meter is broken (not uncommon by the way), get a proper diagnosis and take the prescribed regiment to enhance your self-control.

Sixth, find a healthy surrogate for the thing you tend to overindulge in. People who stop smoking, for example, find success in replacing cigarettes with gum. People who are prone to consuming too many cocktails find success in substituting an alcoholic cocktail with soda water and a small shot of bitters or ginger ale. I knew a guy who was addicted to video games gave them up in favor of playing paint ball. Whatever works for you, substitute a craving or bad habit with a healthy surrogate.

Seventh, change your environment or your friends. This is a tough one, but sometimes you might find yourself in an unhealthy environment, or are too close to others with addictive personalities. We naturally become an extension of the people we associate with the most (another important behavior discussed later in this book). If the common practice of your friends or associates is to "overdo" everything, or take certain things to the extreme on the ill-advised presumption you are "living life to the fullest" well, it might be time to make a change. No job or no social group is worth having if membership requires always having to do something in excess.

Finally, the practice of moderation all comes down to mindfulness and self-discipline. You need to be in touch with who you are and where you are going to avoid the temptations that might take you off course. If you remain mindful of all your senses, the beauty of the world around you, and the special purpose you serve, your inner compass will stay true to what is right and good. Balance is always good.

The Final Word, by Dr. Phil McGraw[4]

" When you choose your behavior, you choose your consequences."

Good reads and resources

Faces of Moderation: The Art of Balance in an Age of Extremes
by Aurelian Craiutu

Benjamin Franklin: 48 Leadership and Life-Changing Lessons from Benjamin Franklin
by Sam Rees

We Have Met the Enemy: Self-Control in an Age of Excess
by Daniel Akst

The Seven Deadly Sins (Classic Reprint)
by James Stalker

The United States of Excess: Gluttony and the Dark Side of American Exceptionalism
by Robert Paarlberg

Her Best-Kept Secret: Why Women Drink-And How They Can Regain Control
by Gabrielle Glaser

Too Much of a Good Thing Is Bad: A Story about Moderation
by Howard Binkow and Reverend Ana

5. Take personal time, rest, reflect and regenerate.

The poet, Maya Angelou, wrote, *"Every person needs to take one day away. A day in which one consciously separates the past from the future. Jobs, family, employers, and friends can exist one day without any one of us, and if our egos permit us to confess, they could exist eternally in our absence. Each person deserves a day away in which no problems are confronted, no solutions searched for. Each of us needs to withdraw from the cares which will not withdraw from us."*

The author of "In Praise of Slowness", Carl Honoré, summarized the importance of this behavior very well, when he wrote, "Our obsession with speed, with cramming more and more into every minute, means that we race through life instead of actually living it. Our health, diet and relationships suffer. We make mistakes at work. We struggle to relax, to enjoy the moment, even to get a decent night's sleep."

True professionals know how to "smell the roses". They know that always being "on" means burning out early. They proactively program rest and relaxation into their lives. They recognize that work-life balance is often touted, but rarely practiced. They use rest and reflection as a competitive weapon. Even though they love their work and derive purpose and energy from it, they are wise enough to know when they should take a break to rest and regenerate. They take time to think about the contributions they want to make and their special place in the world.

What does it mean to take personal time, rest, reflect and regenerate?

As a true professional, you take a day when you need it, not when it conforms to your company's vacation or sick day policies.... not just when it is convenient. You know the difference between stress caused by vision and passion, and stress caused by overwork and anxiety. You feed the former and neutralize the latter with rest and reflection.

You maintain complete control over your life so that you can continue to direct it appropriately. You spend at least a few minutes each day in total silence, calming your thoughts, allowing your subconscious and inner compass to reset themselves. You often take the time to observe the beauty of nature or a work of art.

Unlike many of your peers who suffer from malaise and function at a sub-par level day in and day out, you normally feel rested and energized. You run on all cylinders. You are mindful of what you are working towards and grateful for the opportunity to be on the journey. And although life and work often requires you to have a sense of urgency, in the grand scheme of things, you realize there is no big rush. As Max Ehrmann so eloquently penned in Desiderata:

> Beyond a wholesome discipline, be gentle with yourself.
> You are a child of the universe,
> no less than the trees and the stars;
> you have a right to be here.
> And whether or not it is clear to you,
> no doubt the universe is unfolding as it should.

A true example

One of the cofounders of my second company was tragically killed. He was the technical brains behind a revolutionary new software product we had just brought to market. In the ensuing months, while dealing with our personal grief, my other cofounder and I worked tirelessly to save the company and ensure our friend's legacy. We were miraculously able to stabilize the company and move forward.

For more than three years, we toiled and fought and scrapped together enough investment capital to grow the company. Just when it looked like we would make the big breakthrough, it all came crashing down again. Our investment banker pulled out of a critical funding round at the 11th hour due to their own internal problems. The new programmer we hired to replace our deceased partner sued the company on frivolous grounds in a shameless attempt to extort more money out of us.

Everything seemed lost; it was just too much to overcome this time. With my back against the wall and 20 employees wondering if they would have a job in 30 days, I took time off. I instinctively knew that I needed to get some distance; time to rest, reflect and regenerate. A buddy and I took off on a cross-country motorcycle tour.

There is something about the wide-open road and an ever-changing country-side that is good for the soul. We rode for seven straight days, stopping only when it started getting dark to eat, shower and grab some shuteye. I thought I could go forever...just keep riding...and be perfectly happy. But that is not how life works. The trip gave me plenty of time to think and reflect. My brain began to formulate a plan. By the time we got home, I knew exactly what needed to be done.

A few months later we negotiated the sale of the company to a publicly traded company. We settled the lawsuit with our new programmer: paid him to go away. Some of our employees were hired by the buyer. We gave the others a small severance, wrote letters of recommendation, and helped them get new jobs. It wasn't a huge win as startup success stories go, but it allowed us to live to fight another day. Had I not taken that personal time when I did it might have been a total loss.

Data point

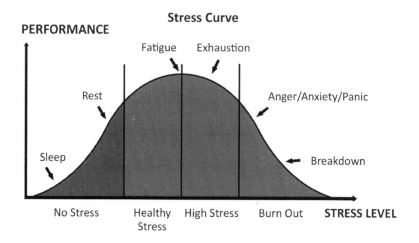

Source: Dr. Krishnan Sivasubramoney, Associate Professor of Psychiatry, Medical College, Thiruvananthapuram, India

A certain amount of stress can be a good thing and increase performance, according to experts. Bad stress, however, decreases performance and can cause health issues. The trick is to monitor your stress levels and find the right balance.

Strategies and tips for taking personal time, resting, reflecting, and regenerating

 So how do you put this adaptive behavior into practice?

First, get away from the hustle, bustle and noise daily. There is power in silence. Being alone with your thoughts, without the distractions of talking heads and commercial messages, gives you time to breathe deeply and clear your mind. In one of the offices I once worked we had a soundproof quiet room. If you don't have a room like that and your office space does not allow you to shut out the noise, find a sanctuary you can escape to regularly.

Second, personal time means totally alone time. No friends, no spouse, no kids or pets. Just you. That means nothing to read and no games or devices to play with. It means quality time with your thoughts, goals and dreams. As silly as it may sound, you need to constantly remind yourself why you are here and what is important to you. It's impossible to keep yourself in perspective if you are always focused on something else.

Third, laugh often and smile a lot. How can you tell happy, reasonably well adjusted people from miserable, unhappy people? Happy people laugh often and smile a lot. They don't take themselves, or the everyday drama of the workplace, too seriously. Read a joke every day, re-watch a video you think is hilarious, or simply slip yourself a sly smile when you contemplate the absurdity of something. There is a certain picture I have in my head, and whenever I conjure it up I burst out laughing. There is no better stress reliever than laughter (okay, maybe one other, *wink*).

Fourth, do not take a vacation that you will need a vacation to recover from. One of the biggest mistakes people make when taking a vacation is cramming in too much, or having unrealistic expectations for how they will feel or what they will experience. Get someplace, settle in and decompress. If you want to do sightseeing or adventure travel, just plan some "downtime" into the schedule. Getting away does not mean flying off to an exotic location. Some of the best, re-energizing vacations, are staycations – stay at home.

Fifth, good conversation leads to new ideas and insights. Shut off the TV, music, devices and other distractions, and simply have an uninterrupted conversation with someone regularly. It can be with your spouse, partner, child, friend, or a new acquaintance. Try to really "hear" what they are saying. Tap into their intelligence, spirit and emotion, and let them tap into yours. Allow them in. It's a great way to unburden and regenerate yourself.

Sixth, life happens. It does no good to deny it or ignore it. Whether it is a personal or family crisis or an unexpected setback at work, keep it in perspective. It's all part of the journey. Trust that things will get better, especially if you take the appropriate action to deal with it. Rest when needed and save yourself for the long run.

Seventh, look outside of yourself and garner personal strength through service to others. Some companies give their employees paid time off to spend time with community organizations. Devote some of your personal time to a worthy cause. I once walked 20 miles for a charity and the next day felt more rested and energized than I was before the walk.

Finally, see your personal relationships as your most prized possession. You are your greatest asset, but your personal relationships are likely your greatest pride and joy. Your life partner, your children, your pets, your dear friends, your trusted coworkers...they are all on their own journeys but they are also one of your best resources for rest and enjoyment. Choose them wisely and be there for them to make the most of your personal time. Rewarding relationships are the ultimate hallmark of personal and professional success.

The Final Word, by Dan Harris[5]

"If you stay in the moment, you'll have what is called spontaneous right action, which is intuitive, which is creative, which is visionary, which eavesdrops on the mind of the universe."

Good reads and resources

5 Steps To Professional Presence: How to Project Confidence, Competence, and Credibility at Work
by Susan Bixler

Wellness on a Shoestring: Seven Habits for a Healthy Life
by Michelle Robin

For This Cause: Finding Purpose Achieving Greatness
by Anthony Thuku Gitonga

In Praise of Slowness: Challenging the Cult of Speed
by Carl Honore

10% Happier: How I Tamed the Voice in My Head, Reduced Stress Without Losing My Edge, and Found Self-Help That Actually Works--A True Story
by Dan Harris

CHAPTER 2

KNOWLEDGEABLE

This is the LEARNED you, how you stay informed and <u>mentally</u> fit.

It's about what you know and don't know, curiosity, reading, ideas and solutions, and continuing education.

6. Know a lot about something and a little about a lot.

Confucius said, *"To know what you know and what you do not know, that is true knowledge."*

The French mathematician and physicist, Blaise Pascal, advised, "Since we cannot know all that there is to be known about anything, we ought to know a little about everything." Perhaps the most sought after behavior of a true professional is his or her knowledge. No enterprise can be run effectively without it, because accurate knowledge drives good decision-making.

The breadth and depth of knowledge possessed by true professionals, not just about their respective professions but of many subjects, is often what distinguishes them from their peers. In almost every profession the people who rise to the top are those who have the best information. They are considered by all who know them to generally be the most knowledgeable.

What does it mean to know a lot about something and a little about a lot?

As a true professional, you possess both specialized knowledge, typically about your chosen profession, and common knowledge, typically universal truths, important historical events and current affairs. You know the difference between knowledge, that which is learned, and wisdom, that which is acquired by experience. You know as much as you can about your job and profession, and because you stay generally well informed about what is going on in the world you have a good perspective on how to practically apply your knowledge. You are both book smart and street smart.

Because you constantly strive for a healthy balance between knowing a lot about something and a little about a lot, you don't have to keep reinventing the wheel. You don't keep making the same mistakes, nor do you rely solely on your raw intelligence. Many of your peers are rich in intelligence, but poor in knowledge. You stay informed, you can converse on a wide variety of topics. You don't just strive to know; you strive to understand. You're a jack of all trades and a master of at least one.

A true example

North Dakota is not generally thought of as the cradle of entrepreneurship. I was sent there in 1985 by my boss, Durward Owen, on a short assignment. I was supposed to be there for six weeks. I stayed for six years. I met the man who would become my new boss and mentor, and help launch my entrepreneurial career.

Bruce Gjovig was the newly-appointed Executive Director of the Center for Innovation and Business Development at the University of North Dakota. He was by far the most well-read person I had ever met at that stage of my life. His depth of knowledge on entrepreneurship, invention and innovation was unparalleled. His books and essays on successful people, particularly American inventors and entrepreneurs, could fill a small library. I put my future into his hands because he knew a lot about what I wanted to be and he was dedicated to the purpose.

There was seemly no topic Bruce Gjovig could not converse about at length. He was involved in state and local politics, and he was on the board of the local art museum. He dragged me to an endless number of industry conferences, community receptions and social events. He knew just about everyone and everything that impacted his center of influence, all in pursuit of a single mission. He was bound and determined to create a center of excellence for the study, development and real world application of entrepreneurship in the state of North Dakota.

To achieve his goal Gjovig had to walk a fine line between university politics, state politics, and private sector support. He successfully raised money from all three. He slowly and methodically, through the rigorous application of actionable knowledge, won the hearts and minds of the men and woman who were in positions of influence to advance his mission.

What impressed me the most was his knowledge of people and their accomplishments. He could work a room better than most politicians. He knew most everything there was to know about every man or woman he met – especially if they were from North Dakota. He knew their stories, their families, their businesses and their achievements. Few people can resist the satisfaction of others recognizing their successes and contributions. After satisfying themselves that he knew what he was talking about and knew what he was doing, it was hard for his friends not to admire him, or his enemies from opposing him.

Today the Center for Innovation at the University of North Dakota is considered one of the best of its kind in the United States.

Data point

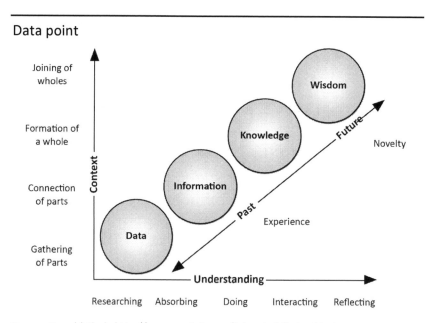

Source: Donald Clark, http://www.nwlink.com/~donclark/index.html

We live in an age where much of the world's knowledge is now accessible via the internet, but a sad fact many people can't distinguish between data, information, knowledge, and wisdom. Scholars have observed we are information rich and knowledge poor. Be a seeker of knowledge, not merely a collector of information. Combined with real-life experiences, it is the path to wisdom.

Strategies and tips for knowing a lot about something and a little about a lot

 So how do you put this adaptive behavior into practice?

First, associate with people who actually know, not those who simply have the job. The Peter Principle states that in every organization people rise to their level of incompetence. Lots of people hold jobs they are not qualified for, or which have outgrown them. It's important for you to recognize the difference, otherwise you will be learning the wrong things from the wrong people. How do you know if one actually knows? Look for the telltale signs covered in the rest of this chapter.

Second, true knowledge must be practiced to be gained. You can read about something all you want. You can listen to tapes and watch endless how-to videos. But to understand it, you must practice it. If you truly know it, you should be able to teach it. Studies prove that we retain 10% of what we read, 20% of what we hear, 30% of what we see, 50% of what we see and hear, 70% of what we share and discuss, 80% of what we experience, and 95% of what we teach others.

Third, be comfortable with the fact that you will never have all the answers. Never be afraid to say, "I don't know." or "I'm not sure." Separate fact from opinion. The path to knowledge often starts with a hypothesis. True knowledge is gained by proving or disproving the hypothesis. Disproving something is not failure, it is knowledge. Thomas Edison said, "I've not failed. I've just found 10,000 ways that won't work."

Fourth, you can't become an expert at something that doesn't hold great interest for you. You don't necessarily have to "love" your field, as some proclaim, but you do have to be keenly interested in it. If you find yourself bored, or not growing, for heaven's sake change professions! Do not be afraid to jump into an entirely new career. Of course, you will want to test it first to make sure it's a good fit. Then set about knowing everything you can about it.

Fifth, stay abreast of major developments in other fields. History is full of examples of major breakthroughs that came from applying knowledge and insights from one field to a completely different field. Subscribe to publications dedicated to covering advancements in other professions. A good strategy is to follow startup news and the stock market. The generations coming up behind you are often the best spotters of new trends.

Sixth, keep up with current events. There are multiple sources which sum up local, national and international news. Browse the headlines at least once a day. Some services will also send you a daily briefing of the topics you are interested in. You should always have a working knowledge of what is going in the world and what your peers and associates are talking about.

Seventh, take up a hobby not related to your work. Many successful professionals take up painting, story writing, playing a musical instrument, crossword puzzles, stamp or coin collecting, or a myriad of other hobbies. Find a hobby that gives you a break from your work, while stimulating your creativity and strengthening your thinking processes. Hobbies also relieve stress and bring you into contact with people you might not ordinarily associate with.

Finally, find a way to make a unique contribution to your profession. Once chosen, focus relentlessly on something you can invent or improve within your field. This drive will force you to learn everything about it. Get as much feedback as you can. Test it in the field, not just on paper. Figure out how to leave a lasting legacy within your chosen profession.

The Final Word, by Fareed Zakaria[6]

"It is likely that human beings will find fulfillment and will be rewarded for the same qualities that they have been rewarded for for 5,000 years. And that is intelligence, hard work, honesty, a sense of character, loyalty to family and friends, and above all, love and faith. If you are trying to decide what you should do, those are the things you should do. And you know it."

Good reads and resources

The Art of Learning: An Inner Journey to Optimal Performance
by Josh Waitzkin

Learning: How To Become a Genius And Expert In Any Subject With Accelerated Learning
by Harvey Segler

Make It Stick: The Science of Successful Learning
by Peter C. Brown and Henry L. Roediger III

Knowledge Encyclopedia Hardcover
by DK (Smithsonian Institution)

Knowledge Stew: The Guide to the Most Interesting Facts in the World, Volume 1
by Daniel Ganninger

The Book of General Ignorance
by John Mitchinson and John Lloyd

Now I Know: The Revealing Stories Behind the World's Most Interesting Facts
by Dan Lewis

Becoming THE Expert: Enhancing Your Business Reputation through Thought Leadership Marketing
by John W. Hayes

Moonwalking With Einstein: The Art and Science of Remembering Everything
by Joshua Foer

The 4-Hour Workweek: Escape 9-5, Live Anywhere, and Join the New Rich
by Timothy Ferriss

7. Be curious, ask a lot of questions and really listen to the answers.

Eleanor Roosevelt summed up the wish of every parent when she remarked, *"I think, at a child's birth, if a mother could ask a fairy godmother to endow it with the most useful gift, that gift should be curiosity."*

Perhaps the biggest curiosity quote blunder of all time was made by Charles H. Duell, the Commissioner of the US patent office in 1899. Mr. Deull infamously uttered these words, *"Everything that can be invented has been invented."* The man was clearly not much of a visionary.

Some of the most famous people in history attribute this one behavior to their success and prosperity. They saw curiosity as something society intentionally or unintentionally drums out of people. They chose to be curious and stay curious. They heeded the words of Albert Einstein: "It is a miracle that curiosity survives formal education."

Curiosity, in particular, is at risk of being lost on the Millennial generation. The fashion designer, Vivienne Westwood, warned, "The age in which we live, this non-stop distraction, is making it more impossible for the young generation to ever have the curiosity or discipline... because you need to be alone to find out anything." Curiosity is a learned behavior. Accomplished people practice it as a conscious choice.

What does it mean to be curious, ask a lot of questions, and really listen to the answers?

As a true professional, you ask a lot of questions and you really listen to the answers. In fact, you pride yourself on being a good listener. The answers prompt you to ask more questions and you keep digging until you get to the root of the matter. You reserve judgment until you discover truth and can discard falsehood. You are good at discerning fact from opinion. You pride yourself on being a bit of a contrarian.

Day in and day out you resist the tendency to be lulled into complacency or dulled by the tedium and distractions of routine. You pay attention to seemingly insignificant daily occurrences. Your favorite word is "why". You love to view yourself as a beginner, because the possibilities are endless: there is always something new to learn and experience.

Even though you know a lot about something, you bristle whenever someone calls you an "expert". You shun know-it-alls. Only ignorant people think they know all there is to know about something. You do not fear the unknowable or the uncertain, you embrace it. You always have more questions, seek more answers. Your mind remains hungry.

A true example

About midway through my career I was working for an innovative software company that would eventually be acquired by Microsoft. The company pioneered the next generation of desktop publishing software by enabling users to seamlessly merge content from disparate sources into a customized, expertly designed document. People loved the product. It set a new standard in automated design of documents and allowed them to be published in any print or electronic form.

While demonstrating the software to an editor of a prominent international publication, she expressed concern about how easy the software would enable users to infringe the copyrights of authors and publishers. I was curious about what she meant and asked her a lot of questions. I only had a cursory understanding of copyright. The answers changed my life. Six months later, I launched iCopyright.com, raised millions of dollars in venture capital, and pioneered the next generation solution for an entirely different industry than the one I was in at the time.

Not only did curiosity lead me to launching a new company, it gave me the ammunition to inspire many others to believe in it, and eventually millions of people to use it. I asked the questions: Why is copyright important and why should ordinary people care about it? What is the copyright symbol? Why is it used? Is it used on all content, on all websites, and in all countries? Does anyone own the copyright symbol?

The answers to those questions enabled us to co-opt the copyright symbol and convince some of the world's largest newspaper and magazine publishers to replace it on their content with the iCopyright symbol. Think about that: the ability to put your company's brand (logo) on millions of web pages. It was akin to seeing today's social media icons on just about every website. At our height we were processing millions of instant copyright permissions every day by having our logo on thousands of other web sites. It all started by being curious about copyright and asking a lot of questions.

Data point

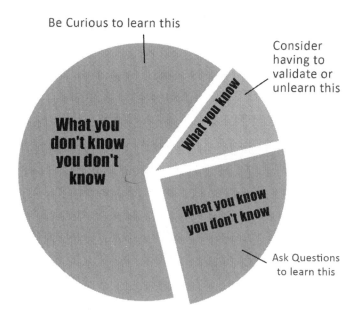

The scary thing about what some people think they know – what they consider knowledge – is actually wrong. Somewhere along the line, they learned something that was simply incorrect, but continue to repeat it and believe it as if it is gospel. Smart people constantly challenge what they think they know and especially what others try to pass off to them as knowledge. Validate. Ask a lot of questions. Be curious. What you don't know you don't know will always vastly outweigh what you think you know.

Strategies and tips for being curious, asking a lot of questions and really listening to the answers

 So how do you put this adaptive behavior into practice?

First, subscribe to question and answer forums. There are several popular online forums where you can ask virtually any question and receive multiple answers. The best answers are "voted up" by others. By just browsing a Q/A forum once or twice a week, even if you post no questions or answers yourself, you will find yourself learning a little about a lot of things.

Second, welcome problems and challenges at work. Seek out manageable risks and uncertainty. These situations force you to be curious, to explore different solutions, and to learn how to become an effective problem-solver. People who embrace uncertainty find more meaning in their personal and professional lives.

Third, look for the unfamiliar in the familiar. On your daily commute, look for something interesting you pass every day, but never paid much attention to before. Stop and visit a shop or restaurant you have never visited before, but see all the time. Observe a coworker's dress or mannerisms, or use a feature in your favorite product or device that you have not tried before.

Fourth, in your staff meetings or conversations with friends or coworkers, try asking the question, "What should I know about you (or about a work-related matter) I don't already know? Or simply say, "Tell me something I don't already know." At one of my companies we played a game to introduce all new employees. They had to tell us two things about themselves that were true and one thing that was false. We could each ask one question, then we all had to guess which thing was false. You learn things about people you would have never known otherwise.

Fifth, read about something that is yet unknowable in mathematics, physics, astronomy, or any other subject that interests you. Thinking about something for which there are no answers reminds you how important it is to be curious. The questions are more important than the answers.

Sixth, after you ask someone a question, listen carefully to the answer, then paraphrase the answer back to them. This practice not only confirms you heard them right so that you can digest and consider their response, it also demonstrates to them that you were listening. Almost everyone can hear, but few people actually listen.

Seventh, when conversing with people, resist the urge to reply immediately or to jump to a conclusion. A true professional waits patiently until others have finished making their point. Rather than replying with an opinion, they often ask another question. One of the most effective tools of a curious person is silence. Let others talk and chatter and debate, while you contemplate. Eventually, they will stop and ask you what you think. Your response will often be the one they will remember most about the discussion.

Finally, allow your curiosity to feed your subconscious while you sleep. Shortly before bed, give your subconscious a question or problem to work on. You can ask yourself, "I wonder why... [state the question]?" Or, "What might be the best way to solve [X]?" Your conscious mind is the source of your curiosity, but it is your subconscious mind that will often lead you to the answers, or at least to more good questions to ask.

The Final Word, by Roy T. Bennett[7]

"Listen with curiosity. Speak with honesty. Act with integrity. The greatest problem with communication is we don't listen to understand. We listen to reply. When we listen with curiosity, we don't listen with the intent to reply. We listen for what's behind the words."

Good reads and resources

Ask It: The Question That Will Revolutionize How You Make Decisions
by Andy Stanley

Curious? Discover the Missing Ingredient to a Fulfilling Life
by Todd Kashdan, PhD

Curious: The Desire to Know and Why Your Future Depends On It
by Ian Leslie

A Curious Mind: The Secret to a Bigger Life
by Brian Grazer and Charles Fishman

Power Questions: Build Relationships, Win New Business, and Influence Others
by Andrew Sobel and Jerold Panas

Leading with Questions: How Leaders Find the Right Solutions by Knowing What to Ask
by Michael J. Marquardt

Good Leaders Ask Great Questions: Your Foundation for Successful Leadership
by John C. Maxwell

8. Read, Read, Read

The famous fashion photographer, David Bailey, said, *"The best advice I ever got was that knowledge is power and to keep reading."*

The most successful people are not just avid readers; they are typically voracious readers. They gain both knowledge and perspective by reading a diverse set of content. They enjoy both fiction and non-fiction. Reading is a staple of their daily diet, no less than food and water. The biographies of accomplished people almost always mention a stack of books by their bedside. Many believed their personal library to be among their most cherished possessions.

What does it mean to Read, Read, Read?

As a true professional, reading is not something you do only once in a while, or when you have to, it's a regular and permanent habit which you have internalized. Reading is automatic. You read for pleasure and for knowledge. No matter what happens in your life or with your job, you face it more confidently, because the joy and knowledge gained from your readings can never be lost or taken away from you.

You read a lot because it stimulates your creativity, expands your vocabulary, and helps you develop concentration and analytical skills. Regular reading also helps you to improve your written and verbal communications skills. You read as much as you can about your profession, especially the latest trends and developments. You regularly scan trade journals and blogs that cover your field. You devour insightful and in-depth analysis on topics which impact your career. You pride yourself on being a well-read professional.

A true example

Growing up in Florida, I was a poor reader as a kid. It pains me to admit it, but I genuinely disliked reading. In retrospect, there were probably two reasons for this. First, reading was not encouraged in my household. My parents never read to me as a child. The only thing I ever saw them read my entire life was the Sunday newspaper. In short, I had no role models to impart the wonders and benefits of reading. I developed no habit for it.

Second, reading was something I was forced to do at school. All those boring text books. The books I was exposed to held no interest for me. In fact, reading was a chore. When my parents forbade me from going outside to play until I finished my homework, I saw reading as a form of punishment. It was something I was forced to do, so I always did it with great haste and distaste.

It wasn't until my second year in high school that I read a book cover-to-cover I actually enjoyed. My English Literature teacher assigned the class *Adventures of Huckleberry Finn.* Later in the year he assigned *To Kill a Mockingbird.* I enjoyed both books, but I labored through them. I was a *very slow* reader. It took me three times longer than my peers to finish those books. It reinforced the notion in my mind that reading was not for me. A self-fulfilling prophecy can be a bad thing.

After graduating high school, I was torn between going to college or joining the military. My dad, who was a veteran of the Korean war, talked me into going to college. He wisely advised, "A college education will give you more choices in life."

My grades and my budget were not sufficient to attend a four-year university, so I registered for classes at the local community college. A love of reading and good study habits are fundamental to a college education. I had neither; I flunked out the first semester. It was then and there that I realized how far behind I was and, if I didn't fix it, I would likely be relegated to a career which would not allow me to fulfill my full potential.

It took me six years to get through college. My strategy was to take less than a full load each semester so that I did not get overwhelmed as I had my first semester. One of the things that saved me was being a good note taker. I never missed classes and took copious notes. In short, I simply applied myself.

My reading skills improved over time. Reading is like any other skill: the more you do it the better you get. I learned there are different ways to read material depending upon whether I was doing it for work, study, or pleasure; immersion or summary. I bought a lot of Cliffs Notes; abbreviated versions of books.

By the time I went to work for Durward in my first full-time job I was a reasonably proficient reader. I could read and comprehend as fast as most of my coworkers. But it was under Durward's tutelage that I developed reading as a lifetime habit. As silly as it sounds, I thought I was largely done with reading. My formal education was behind me; I no longer had to read. Durward quickly dissuaded me of that silly notion. His mantra to all his employees was this: you will read at least one newspaper per day, one trade journal per week, and one book per month. And we all did...and I still do to this day.

Data point

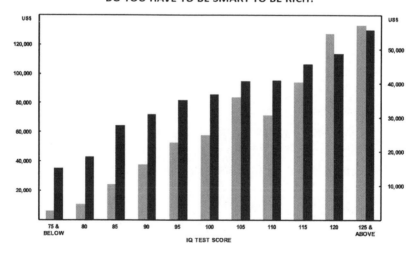

DO YOU HAVE TO BE SMART TO BE RICH?

Source: BCA Research

Social scientists cite studies that prove you do NOT have to be smart to become rich. I guess it all depends on what one considers "smart." There are studies which show there is a direct correlation between one's IQ and his or her income and net worth. Here's what I have learned by observing successful people: The more you read, the smarter you get. The smarter you get, the more money you make. The more money you make, the more money you are likely to keep. Improving your vocabulary and cognitive skills will definitely help you earn and retain wealth.

Strategies and tips for reading, reading, reading

 So how do you put this internalized behavior into practice?

First, develop the art of skimming. Whether for work or pleasure, not every publication needs to be read word-for-word. Skim headlines, sub-headlines, call-outs, and summaries. Get into the habit of quickly distilling the essence of the material. Save in-depth reading for important, high-value content.

Second, stop reading something that is badly written, unsatisfying, or a waste of time. At home, there is no law saying you must finish a book. If it doesn't engage you after a few chapters, toss it aside and pick up another. At work, send the piece back to whomever sent it to you and ask them to re-write it, or summarize the key points. In the companies I ran my employees needed to keep all memos to one page and every email needed to identify the objective and action required in the first sentence.

Third, always carry a good book or industry whitepaper and get in the habit of reading it anywhere and anytime. This is super easy to do today with digital devices. Whenever you have downtime you can always do a bit of reading, if only for 5-10 minutes. Whether you are on a bus, waiting to see the doctor, or standing in line to order coffee you can always sneak in a few paragraphs.

Fourth, highlight or underline salient points as you read. This helps your brain to retain the information. This practice also helps you to quickly go back and pull out the data you want to follow up on. If necessary, rip out the pages of the stuff you need to act upon. This practice always aggravates me when others do it with publications intended to be publicly shared, like with airline magazines. "But hey," I think to myself. "Whatever they found that was so important just might change their life, or the trajectory of their company." Good for them!

Fifth, join a book club, or dissect work-related content with coworkers. I've been a member of several book clubs over the years. I always enjoyed hearing other people's perspectives about the books we shared. At work, I would often assign my managers an industry-related book, trade article, or whitepaper, then assemble them to discuss their findings and perspectives.

Sixth, keep a reading "wish list" and a few good books on your nightstand. Whenever your night stand starts running low, pull up your wish list and order one or two books off the top. Whenever you are attending a conference or dining with a colleague and a good book is recommended, write it down! Better yet, do what I do: log on to the net with your mobile device and order it on the spot.

Seventh, try audio books or podcasts. Earlier in my career I listened to a book on the way to and from work every day. I especially love book summary audio casts. They enable me to consume the essence of four or five books in the time it would normally take to read one book.

Finally, read an important article or work related memo aloud. There is something about hearing yourself recite the words which helps you become intimate with them. In this same vein, try writing a book review and posting it on the page where others are considering buying the book. Writing a review or summary of the book also helps you retain the story and converse about it with your associates. *Shameless plug: Please review this book!*

The Final Word, by Fran Lebowitz[8]

"Think before you speak. Read before you think."

Good reads and resources

Speed Reading: The Comprehensive Guide To Speed Reading - Increase Your Reading Speed By 300% In Less Than 24 Hours
by Nathan Armstrong

How to Read a Book: The Classic Guide to Intelligent Reading
by Mortimer J. Adler and Charles Van Doren

Speed Reading: How to Dramatically Increase Your Reading Speed & Become
the Top 1% of Readers - Read Faster, Learn Better
by Michelle Lawton

Hacking Literacy: 5 Ways To Turn Any Classroom Into a Culture Of Readers
by Gerard Dawson

Ever Wonder Why?: Here Are the Answers!
by Douglas B. Smith

9. Have more than one idea
and at least two solutions to every problem.

One of the most popular and respected authors on emotional intelligence (EQ), Travis Bradberry, wrote, *"Influencers inspire everyone around them to explore new ideas and think differently about their work."*

Perhaps the most poignant words on this subject are from the former U.S. Four-Star General and Secretary of State, Colin Powell: "Great leaders are almost always great simplifiers, who can cut through argument, debate and doubt, to offer a solution everybody can understand."

Accomplished people remain versatile when it comes to offering new ideas and suggesting possible solutions to problems. They do not have a fixed mindset; only one approach or one solution to a challenge or problem. They heed the wisdom of Aristotle, who said, "Nothing is more dangerous than a man with one idea."

True professionals have an open mindset. They always offer multiple approaches and solutions. Using their knowledge, training and experience, they are always ready with options...always open to the possibilities. After all is considered and debated, true professionals can clearly articulate the options in a way which helps their superiors and their subordinates choose a viable path.

What does it mean to have more than one idea and at least two solutions to every problem?

As a true professional, you can be depended upon to look at a question or problem from multiple angles. You offer several answers, not just the first, most obvious answer. If you don't have good answers because you don't have enough information at the moment, you are ready with some ideas on where and how to get the answers. Most importantly, you never, ever, bring a problem without a possible solution.

When challenges and problems arise at work, as they always do, you can frame them clearly and then suggest multiple ways to tackle them. You don't allow yourself to fall in love with any one idea or solution because you realize becoming attached to a single idea or solution may cause it to become your next problem.

You love to brainstorm and riff, feeding off others' ideas and stream of consciousness. Whether it is helping to come up with new products or features, ways to attract more customers or donors, or instituting new processes, you encourage input from others. Things are rarely black or white to you. Because you have trained yourself to always have more than one idea and multiple solutions to every problem, you can often be counted on to come up with something no one else has thought of.

A true example

One of my first companies manufactured computerized kiosks. We placed them in high traffic public locations like airports, malls, and hotel lobbies. They were quite the novelty in those days. People used the kiosks by pressing four big buttons to navigate through a menu of options and print directions and coupons. The kiosks were powered by large personal computers programmed using floppy disks. We made money by selling advertising to local merchants. Every merchant in town received a basic listing for free, but if they wanted a big color ad or coupon which users could print, they paid a monthly fee.

The problem with the business model was that ad sales barely covered the cost of manufacturing and maintenance. It could take a year or more to recover the cost of each kiosk. The printers would jam and run out of paper. The kiosks would often need to be rebooted after a power outage or electrical spike. Every time we sold a new ad the kiosks had to be updated in person by floppy disk. Even after recovering the cost of manufacturing the kiosk itself, the maintenance and support costs of servicing the computers and printers was killing us. We needed to solve this problem. We needed viable ideas on how to reduce costs and increase profits.

My idea was to change the business model. I proposed we sell the kiosks to the facilities: the airports, malls and hotels, and then split the ad revenue with them. That way we would cover most of the costs of manufacturing upfront. The facilities loved our kiosks because they provided valuable services to their guests and visitors. Our electronic concierge could replace a human concierge, plus give the facility a way to make money from a share of the advertising revenue. I was convinced this was the path forward.

After weeks of research, number crunching and debate among my team, I called them together to call the vote. I needed everyone's buy-in to change direction. After making the case (again), I thought I had consensus, but then our Chief Technology Officer spoke up. "Why do we need to make the kiosks at all?" he asked. He threw a popular computer magazine on the table. The cover story extolled the coming revolution in multimedia computing. "We are not in the kiosk business," he said. "We are in the multimedia software business."

I was immediately defensive because I had no idea what that meant. My vision was thousands of kiosks in public locations across the country. Every time I flew out of an airport or stayed in a hotel, I dreamed of seeing "my kiosks" in each of them one day. Our CTO was undaunted. "Let others make the kiosks. We will sell them the software to power it and relieve ourselves of the costs and burdens of manufacturing and maintenance."

This is what is known today as "The Pivot", what smart startup companies do to survive and grow when their original product or business model is not working.

It took me a while to "get it", but it ended up saving the company and propelling us in a new and better direction. The software could not only power kiosks, it could allow others to create computer-based training (CBT) programs and multimedia business presentations. We literally created the forerunner to PowerPoint. The applications for our software were numerous, for many different markets, not just for powering kiosks. The packaging costs were a few dollars, as opposed to tens of thousands of dollars to manufacture kiosks. The margins were outrageous.

Thanks to my CTO having more than one idea and multiple solutions to how we could reduce costs and increase profits, we became a pioneer of the multi-media software industry and built a company which lasted for 10 years.

Data point

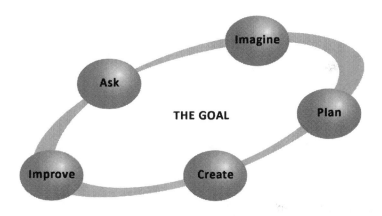

Source: Christine Cunningham of the Museum of Science in Boston

Ideation and problem-solving involve a similar process. The first step is to be clear about the goal. Ask, "What am I solving for?" The second step is to ask a lot of questions to flesh out the requirements and required data inputs. The third step is to imagine and brainstorm all sorts of possible solutions. The fourth step is to make some assumptions and investigate their feasibility. The fifth step is to plan, create and implement the solution. The final step is to continually improve the solution based on measurable metrics and results.

Strategies and tips for having more than one idea and multiple solutions to every problem

 So how do you put this adaptive behavior into practice?

First, understand ideas are about connecting the dots. Ideas are concepts that lie between two things and connect those things together, sometimes in new and surprising ways. These connections allow you to see things which might not be obvious to others. The first step is to think about how the "thing" you are contemplating is connected to other things. All those connection points are ideas. When you connect A with B, that's one idea, but when you connect A with C, that's an entirely different idea. What is a recipe? It's putting together different ingredients in certain portions to create a unique drink or a dish. The same ingredients are used in hundreds of dishes, but each unique combination creates a different taste.

Second, write down ideas as they come to you, or record them using your mobile phone. People who always seem to have good ideas are in the habit of keeping a notebook. They jot down their thoughts without making judgments about them, or trying to bring them to any particular conclusion. Later, they review them and often make surprising connections.

Third, brainstorm and riff with your friends and coworkers about possible solutions to problems. The connections they make will lead you to see even more connections. Each person brings his or her own knowledge and experience to ideation. Great ideas are seldom the product of one mind. They are the product of many minds working together.

Fourth, get in the habit of testing and validating ideas, no matter how undeveloped. You can, of course, search the Internet to explore what knowledge and experience others have with the issue. It's also a good practice to talk to others and ask them questions about their frustrations and experiences. In the middle of a dull conversation with others, I have gotten in the habit of changing the trajectory of the conversation by simply asking, "So, have you ever had the problem of XYZ?" This question often leads to a stimulating riff.

Fifth, be wary of confirmation bias, the tendency to interpret initial findings or opinions of others as confirmation of your beliefs or theories. We all want to hear what we want to hear. We tend to block out evidence that may disagree with our ideas. This is something you should be super conscious about. Ask yourself and others the question, "How might this idea or solution be wrong?" There are usually more reasons not to act on an idea than there are to act on it. That does not mean you should not act. It just means you are proceeding with eyes wide open on why or how it might not be right, but could at least lead you to what's right.

Sixth, get away from familiar surroundings. New ideas and solutions rarely come when going to the same places and doing the same routine day in and day out. That is why "off sites" are so important to organizations. Get away from the office. Sometimes, you need to get away from the people you always hang out with. Nothing stimulates the creative juices more than all new places, people and experiences. If you're bold enough, take a pilgrimage to a different country. Novel sights, sounds, tastes, cultures and experiences will light new fires in your brain and create all-new connections.

Seventh, establish success markers and have a Plan B. Whatever solution you choose you should set some markers that provide early indication of a probable successful outcome. No solution should be permanent. Define in advance what metrics or outcomes define success, and within what timeframe. If you are not on track with the desired outcomes, you can go to Plan B.

Finally, visualize or prototype possible solutions. Some ideas sound great. They look good on paper, in words. But when you chart them, graph them, draw them, prototype them…. visualize them, you may find serious flaws. One of the reasons white boards are so popular in the work environment is because they help get ideas out of your head and into the physical world, where they can be visualized and better understood. I knew an inventor who sculpted his inventions in clay before building them.

The Final Word, by Theodore Rubin[9]

"The problem is not that there are problems. The problem is expecting otherwise and thinking that having problems is a problem."

Good reads and resources

Become An Idea Machine: Because Ideas Are The Currency Of The 21st Century
by Claudia Azula Altucher and James Altucher

A Technique for Producing Ideas: The simple, five-step formula anyone can use to be more creative in business and in life!
by James Webb Young

Where Good Ideas Come From: The Natural History of Innovation
by Steven Johnson

Sprint: How to Solve Big Problems and Test New Ideas in Just Five Days
by Jake Knapp and John Zeratsky

Thinking, Fast and Slow
by Daniel Kahneman

Unlimited Memory: How to Use Advanced Learning Strategies to Learn Faster, Remember More and be More Productive
by Kevin Horsley

Sprint: How to Solve Big Problems and Test New Ideas in Just Five Days
by Jake Knapp and John Zeratsky

The Art of Problem Solving, Vol. 1 and 2: And Beyond Solutions Manual
by Richard Rusczyk and Sandor Lehozcky

Innovation and Entrepreneurship
by Peter F. Drucker

10. Never stop learning, approach a profession as a continuing education.

Oprah Winfrey is one of the most successful television hosts, actresses, producers and media magnates of all time. She said, *"I am a woman in process. I'm just trying like everybody else. I try to take every conflict, every experience, and learn from it. Life is never dull."*

B eing a life-long learner is a pivotal behavior of all true professionals. They see their formal education as just the beginning, a foundation to build upon. Most will credit an insatiable thirst for more knowledge as one of the reasons for their successes.

One of the secrets of accomplished people is realizing they must "unlearn" certain things which were taught to them by their parents, peers or instructors, once proven to be inaccurate or outdated. Very little knowledge is universal and unchanging. Knowledge is ever-evolving, and so must be every professional's capacity and determination for continued education. Henry Ford extolled, "Anyone who stops learning is old, whether at twenty or eighty. Anyone who keeps learning stays young."

True professionals are always "approaching" their professions. They never feel as if they ever completely arrive. There is more to know and learn than can be attained in any one lifetime. They share the philosophy of Mahatma Gandhi, who said, "Live as if you were to die tomorrow. Learn as if you were to live forever."

What does it mean to never stop learning and to approach a profession as a continuing education?

As a true professional, you can never know enough about your job or your industry. You eagerly accept new training offered, or the opportunity to attend workshops, conferences and tradeshows. You spend a little time on your own outside of work each week to peruse blogs, white papers, and online learning programs. As previously covered in this chapter, you read a lot and you ask a lot of questions.

Over time you develop the habit of being a self-directed learner. You don't have to be prompted or incentivized, you have internalized continual learning. In a way, learning is like oxygen to you. You exhale the knowledge previously acquired and inhale fresh, new knowledge and ideas to keep your brain engaged and your spirit energized.

If you are really dedicated, you find mentors who can impart both new knowledge and strategies for how to apply it effectively. You are not daunted by any learning curve. You break new content into manageable and digestible pieces, then study it at a pace that is comfortable until you understand it.

A true example

Ageism is a pervasive, equal opportunity discrimination practice in the workforce. Unlike sexism, racism, creedism, and every other 'ism, each worker on the planet eventually becomes a victim. We are all going to be "old" sooner or later. Ageism is practiced by employers who push out aging workers in favor of younger workers who will work harder and longer for less money. Aging workers also fall victim to ageism because they "age out" mentally. Their skills get rusty and their knowledge becomes stale and ineffective due to the rapid pace of technological change and an ever-evolving global economy.

You might be thinking, "I'm young, I've just started my career, I don't have to worry about ageism for a long time." You would be wrong. In many professions workers can "age out" mentally by the time they are 35 years old, or they simply become complacent and fall behind. Computer programming is one such profession.

David was 33 years old and in high demand. The Internet boom was just getting started and there was a dearth of good computer programmers, particularly those who knew ecommerce. He had worked at several of the large high-tech companies in Seattle and Silicon Valley. He had a stellar resume and good references. I thought I was lucky to get him. He was given a six-figure salary and generous stock options. His job was to develop the ecommerce module for our new internet service.

One month before we were scheduled to launch, my Director of Engineering informed me we would not make the deadline. The product was not ready; specifically, the ecommerce module. I was livid because the engineering team had plenty of time and were all well-paid. I was in the middle of raising another round of financing from venture capitalists. Missing our launch would jeopardize the raise and put the company at a competitive disadvantage because we were in a race to market. We would lose our "first mover" advantage. I demanded to know what caused the holdup. He looked at me matter of factly and replied, "David doesn't know his sh*t."

As it turned out, David had initially tried to write the code using an outdated programming language and old libraries. When the Director of Engineering found out about it, he told David he would need to develop the ecommerce module using the same platform as the rest of the team. David said, "no problem" and went back to work.

David was unable to come up to speed and didn't even try. He often did not come in to the office, saying he could get more done at home. He wrote no code whatsoever. After he was terminated for cause, he filed a complaint with the department of labor and industries and sued me for wrongful termination. I had to pay him a significant sum of money to go away so I would not be distracted from the task at hand, which was saving the company. Later I found out he had pulled the same stunt at his previous employer.

This is a case where David simply stopped learning. He failed to keep up with the latest developments in his field. Rather than doing the work to keep his skills and knowledge current he devised a four-prong strategy: bluff, stall, sue and settle. That's a no-win strategy in the long run. I have no idea what David is doing these days, but I know it isn't computer programming and I doubt he is even working in the high tech industry any longer. On many levels, he was not a lifelong learner.

This is also a case where I failed. I did not know what I did not know when I hired David. I did not know how to vet him properly. We were running fast and snatching up any tech talent we could. I had hired David before I hired his boss, which is a bad practice. People who know should hire other people who know, especially if they are going to be direct reports. No professional deserves to be saddled with an incompetent staff. That one was on me. I learned never to do it again.

Data point

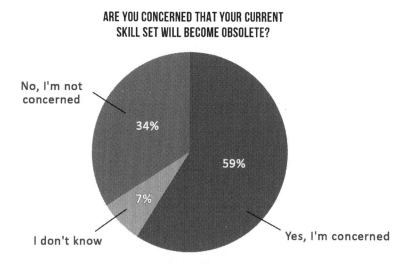

ARE YOU CONCERNED THAT YOUR CURRENT SKILL SET WILL BECOME OBSOLETE?

No, I'm not concerned — 34%

7%

59%

I don't know

Yes, I'm concerned

Source: Tech Pro Research

Technology continues to increase the pace of change in all industries. Best practices are always evolving. True professionals know their best chance of staying competitive is to continue their education and to upgrade their skills.

You can bet the 34% who are not concerned and the 7% who don't know in this survey, won't likely remain competitive in their professions.

Strategies and tips for continuing education

 So how do you put this internalized behavior into practice?

First, use a news alert service to receive daily or weekly posts on developments in your field. There are several good services; most are free of charge. Define topics and keywords relevant to your industry or profession. The service will scour the web each day and bring you items which are relevant. We live in a day and age where knowledge now comes to us. We no longer must go seek it.

Second, become an apprentice or volunteer for a leader in an adjacent industry. No industry or profession is an island. They are all dependent upon or influenced by adjacent industries or professions. Getting exposure to an adjacent industry breeds cross-pollination. It will help you see your own field in a new light. You will acquire new knowledge and insights you can apply to your work.

Third, seek the limelight in your profession to keep yourself sharp. Share your knowledge on social media and online forums. Ask for feedback. The act of putting yourself out there to public scrutiny forces you to know your stuff. For example, I post weekly to several professional forums. I usually need to do 3-4 hours of research and fact checking before I post. Sharing is caring and a healthy discipline for continual learning.

Fourth, get certified. Your profession probably offers a variety of certifications which demonstrate you are up to date with best practices. You can also take skills tests offered by third party associations and freelance marketplaces. When posting your resume or professional profile, it never hurts to have a few letters after your name that tells the world what credentials you hold.

Fifth, if you are not already a "positive deviant (PD)", find one to hang out with. A PD is one whose unconventional thinking and strategies enable them to find better solutions than their peers, despite being in similar circumstances and having no extra resources or knowledge than their peers. PD's see the world differently and inspire learning.

Sixth, don't forget to work on soft skills. It's not just about knowing more; it's about how you use your knowledge to influence your peers and improve your profession and workplace. Soft skills mean people skills, management skills and leadership skills. It's not enough to just know about your profession, you must know about people and how to work effectively with them.

Seventh, do whatever you need to do to put yourself in a learning culture. If you are not constantly learning at work, quit now! If learning is not part of your organization's culture, you either need to change the culture or change organizations. Life is too short to go stale too quickly. Find a work environment which continues to challenge you.

Finally, keep yourself in perspective. Know *why* you are always learning and to what end. Stay sharp not out of fear, but out of hope. As Socrates said, "The unexamined life is not worth living." Knowledge is also knowing oneself. Never stop learning so you may always remain true to yourself.

The Final Word, by Malala Yousafzai[10]

"All I want is education and I am afraid of no one."

Good reads and resources

Mind Games: The Aging Brain and How to Keep it Healthy
by Kathleen Harmeyer and Kathryn Wetzel

Mindset: The New Psychology of Success
by Carol S. Dweck

Emotional Agility: Get Unstuck, Embrace Change, and Thrive in Work and Life
by Susan David

Emotional Intelligence 2.0
by Travis Bradberry and Jean Greaves

How To Keep Your Mind Sharp - Even If You're 90!
by Anthony Metivier

The Art of Possibility: Transforming Professional and Personal Life
by Rosamund Stone Zander and Benjamin Zander

Off Balance: Getting Beyond the Work-Life Balance Myth to Personal and Professional Satisfaction
by Matthew Kelly

Reaching Your Potential: Personal and Professional Development
by Robert K. Throop and Marion B. Castellucci

CHAPTER 3

CONNECTED

This is the SOCIAL you, how you leverage people and <u>collaborate</u> with your associates.

It's about networking, joining and contributing, close companions, choosing your associates wisely, and engaging with others.

11. Develop a professional network and enroll others in your dreams and goals.

Meg Jay wrote an insightful book for Millennials entitled: <u>The Defining Decade: Why Your Twenties Matter--And How to Make the Most of Them Now</u>. She wrote, *"It's the people we hardly know, and not our closest friends, who will improve our lives most dramatically."*

Most accomplished people will proudly tell you they know a lot of other people; mostly a lot of other accomplished people. Most will also admit to having achieved at least some of their success by going through the doors which were opened for them by prominent people in their professional network. They, in turn, become well-known among their peers and help open doors for others.

The movers and shakers in every industry tend to flock together and associate with one another. A true professional knows how to *use people* in a positive and reciprocal manner. Michele Jennae, a professional coach, tells her clients, "Networking is not about just connecting people. It's about connecting people with people, people with ideas, and people with opportunities." This is great advice for developing a professional network and enrolling others in your dreams and goals.

What does it mean to develop a professional network and enroll others in your dreams and goals?

As a true professional, you make it a regular practice to reach out to peers and colleagues who are in your profession, or who can refer people in a position to advance your goals. You believe in people power: the more powerful people you know, the more powerful you become. You don't just post your professional profile online and willy nilly invite others to connect with you. It's not about how many connections you have, but the value of those connections. To you, a connection is not merely a name and a title, he or she is a valued relationship.

Most of the people in your professional network not only know who you are and what you do, they know your aspirations. You proactively enroll them in your dreams and goals. You invite them to share their aspirations with you and ask them how you can help them on their journey. As a true professional, you see your network as a two-way street. You seek to give, not only receive, and you know you can only achieve your dreams and goals by helping others to achieve theirs.

A true example

Proactive professional networking has always been a staple of my professional career. It was drilled into my head by my first boss, Durward Owen. He required his staff to attend every industry conference, where we would meet and develop relationships with our peers. Durward even dragged us to operas and symphonies, not only to expose us to more refined arts than we were accustomed to, but because he knew we would "bump into" successful people who could help us with the next phase of our careers.

Rather than recite one of the many stories about how traditional networking created an amazing opportunity for me, as it has for countless other professionals, I thought you might enjoy a story about how to quickly build a professional network using a head fake.

In the age of the Internet and social media, professional networking has moved online. People connect with others virtually, share their knowledge and connections, collaborate, and get to know others without ever meeting them in person. The largest web service that facilitates these connections is Linkedin, with more than 450 million users. Like everyone else I had a basic profile on Linkedin and had connected to many of the people whom I knew or had previously done business with; a little more than 500 people. I knew, however, that to avoid going stale and to continue to build a strong network I would need to master this new online tool.

To do that I wrote and published an article on Linkedin entitled, "Why I Won't Accept Your Linkedin Invitation". That's where the head fake comes in. I set out to build a stronger network by telling people why I wouldn't network with them. Many people had a strong, visceral reaction to the article, both positively and negatively. Within a few months more than one million people had read the article; more than 20,000 thousand "liked" it and more than 8,000 people felt compelled to comment on it. My professional network grew tenfold from 500 people to more than 5,000 people in less than one year.

You might be thinking I ignored my own advice by willy nilly accepting everyone's invitation. In fact, I received more than 15,000 requests to connect. I only accepted one in three. I thoughtfully considered every single request, reviewed every profile, and often exchanged an email or phone call with the people who wanted to connect with me. Some of them became new friends and colleagues. I have enrolled many of them in my dreams and goals, or the dreams and goals of my clients. Likewise, I know the dreams and goals of many of the people in my network and am always looking for opportunities to assist them.

What's the moral of this story? First, people don't want to associate with just anyone. They want to be selective and they want YOU to be selective about whom you associate with. They feel special if they are among the professionals you thoughtfully invited to be part of your network. You need to TELL THEM and SHOW THEM you value them. Second, you can build a new and better network at any stage of your career. Seriously, the people you are connected to right now may not be relevant to you, or you to them, in five years. A network is not a static thing; it is a dynamic thing. People will always be coming and going in and out of your life and career. You must always be growing and pruning your professional network.

Data point

Concentric Value of a Professional Network

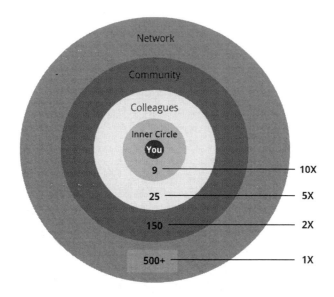

Source: How to Increase the Value of Your Professional Network by 10X, Michael O'Donnell

Think of your professional network as being four concentric circles, with you at the center. Your inner circle should deliver you 10x the value of your outer circle. Think carefully about who you invite to be in which circle. See strategies three – six below for tips on how to maximize the value of your professional network.

Strategies and tips for developing a professional network and enrolling others in your dreams and goals.

 So how do you put this adaptive behavior into practice?

First, carry business cards at all times, or install a mobile app that allows you to transfer your business card to another mobile phone wirelessly. You

never know who you might run into. I've met valuable contacts standing in line at the coffee shop.

Second, upon being given a business card from a new connection, immediately drop them a note and extend an invitation to connect with you on your favorite social media or professional networking site. HINT: offer to introduce them to someone you know who might be helpful to them, or send them an article or other information they might find useful. If you want to make a lasting impression and build solid relationships, deliver value to every new connection immediately. Don't ask for nor expect anything in return; it will come in due time.

Third, at least once per year, reorganize the people in your professional network into four concentric rings based on what you want to accomplish over the next 12-18 months, as follows:

a. Inner Circle – these are your allies and closest compadres. Research shows the ideal number is 9, but no more than 12. These people are mission-critical to your success in the next 12 months.

b. Colleagues – these are the movers and shakers in your space. They are your peers and your mentors. They have deep knowledge and strong connections you can leverage. Research shows the ideal number of close colleagues you can reasonably maintain strong and reciprocal relationships with is between 20 and 25.

c. Community – these are likeminded people who share similar goals, aspirations, and interests. They are your tribe. They are probably already organized around interest groups and forums. The number of people in your community should be about 150. This is often referred to as Dunbar's Number: the maximum number you can have to maintain stable relationships.

d. Network – these are the people in your extended network. Those on Linkedin, Twitter, Google+, Facebook (for companies), Instagram, Vine, etc. This is the total pool of people you can draw from to pull into your more valuable, concentric rings, depending upon your current circumstances.

This exercise should be done at least annually. People will move in and out of these rings. You should always be adding to your network (the outer ring) and promoting people to your inner rings, or demoting people within the inner rings back to the outer rings. Your life and career are not stagnant; so, neither should be your professional network. To maximize its value, it needs to be fluid and dynamic.

Fourth, rank the key touch points you have with the people within your concentric rings, then use those rankings to foster, enhance and maintain those relationships. Touch points are things like meetings in person, phone calls, email exchanges, online chats, etc. Focus on the connections you have the best touch points with. This exercise also helps to inform which of your connections should be in which rings.

Fifth, increase the number of "gives" to those in your network in proportion to which ring they fall within. Judiciously monitor the number of "asks" in the same proportion. Those in your inner circle need a lot of love, and you should expect a lot of love from them in return. Healthy relationships are about give and take. If you have ever been in a one-sided relationship, you know it is not very rewarding.

Sixth, a strong professional network is governed by the law of reciprocity. Always be looking to give and don't hesitate to ask in equal proportions. Those who repeatedly do not reciprocate should be demoted to the outer rings. Those that reciprocate, or give without asking, should be promoted to your inner rings, especially if what they give advances your 12-18 month goals.

Seventh, perform a "balance of trade audit" on the referrals you made and received for the year. You should know the relative value you have delivered to those in your inner circle and the relative value they have delivered to you. If the value of their referrals were lower (or non-existent) than the value of the referrals you made to them, they have a trade deficit. If the value of their referrals were greater than those you made to them, they have a trade surplus. Try to balance your referral accounts each year.

Finally, clearly communicate your goals to the most important and influential people in your professional network at least once per year. Naturally, keep it real. You might want to be a billionaire by the time you are 30, but most of your connections are not going to be inspired by your quest for riches. They will be inspired by your aspirations to better yourself and others. Send them a New Year letter and let them know what you accomplished in the previous year and what you are looking forward to doing in the coming year. Ask them to share their aspirations with you!

The Final Word, by Kate White[11]

"If you've just had a brief conversation at an event, ask, "Is it all right if I drop you a note?" You can follow up with a question in writing. Also, periodically send your potential mentor or sponsor information that she will find insightful. When you have an accomplishment under your belt, let her know about it."

Good reads and resources

Never Eat Alone: And Other Secrets to Success, One Relationship at a Time
by Keith Ferrazzi and Tahl Raz

How to Win Friends & Influence People
by Dale Carnegie

Networking Is Not Working: Stop Collecting Business Cards and Start Making Meaningful Connections
by Derek Coburn

The Defining Decade: Why Your Twenties Matter--And How to Make the Most of Them Now
by Meg Jay

Always Know What To Say - Easy Ways To Approach And Talk To Anyone
by Peter W. Murphy

I Shouldn't Be Telling You This: Success Secrets Every Gutsy Girl Should Know
by Kate White

How to Talk to Anyone: 92 Little Tricks for Big Success in Relationships
by Leil Lowndes

12. Join and contribute to professional, community, charitable and social organizations.

Caroline Kennedy said of her father, John F. Kennedy, *"I feel that my father's greatest legacy was the people he inspired to get involved in public service and their communities, to join the Peace Corps, to go into space. And really that generation transformed this country in civil rights, social justice, the economy and everything."*

True professionals know they are not an island. They do not exist in a vacuum and cannot stand alone. Their growth and development depends upon them associating with likeminded people. Their progress requires them to join and contribute to organizations which foster their development and support the greater good. True professionals quickly learn involvement in a variety of organizations outside of their chosen profession leads to serendipitous encounters which end up changing their lives for the better.

What does it mean to join and contribute to professional, community, charitable and social organizations?

As a true professional you belong to at least one professional association. Upon joining a professional association, you look for ways to participate and contribute. You chair a committee or volunteer to help out at industry events. You get to know the leadership because you know they are in a position to help you grow professionally and advance your career. The active people within your profession know the people you need to know, and you are more likely to meet them by getting involved.

It's not all about work related memberships. You reserve some bandwidth for people and causes outside of your work. You volunteer at your church, a community mission, or charitable organization. You may donate blood on occasion, or raise money for a worthy charity by participating in marathons, walk-a-thons, bike-a-thons, or other fundraising events. You try to experience and participate in the world outside of your own little world. Although not directly related to your work, you believe those experiences enable you to become a better professional; a true professional.

A true example

Like most people in their 20's who were just starting their careers, I could barely pay my rent and put food on the table. I didn't make much money and was paying off student loans. I thought of myself as my favorite charity. Surely, no one could expect me to give to charity when I could barely support myself?

In his usual direct style, my first boss Durward Owen told me in no uncertain terms, "You not only need to volunteer, you will start this week." One of Durward's favorite sayings was, "Service to others is but the rent we pay to occupy space while here on Earth." The great prize fighter, Muhammad Ali, said the same thing slightly differently: "Service to others is the rent you pay for your room here on earth."

To my boss and task master, Durward Owen, it did not matter how broke or busy I was. He insisted everyone who worked for him must "look outside of themselves". I signed up to be a "Big Brother" for Big Brothers Big Sisters of America. I was only 24 years old. I had never done anything like that before. It turned out to be a memorable and rewarding experience for me as well as my young charge. So began a lifelong practice of joining and contributing.

Over the years I have been a member of a variety of organizations. Each one contributed to my growth and development in different ways. As a software company executive, I was a member of the Software and Information Industry Association (SIIA), where I chaired several committees. As an entrepreneur, I was a member of the Northwest Entrepreneur's Organization (NWEN), where I became Chairman of the Board. As a member of ClubCorp, I was affiliated with more than 200 clubs in 26 states, where many of the movers and shakers in every major U.S. market are members.

Not only have these associations contributed to my professional development, they are responsible for bringing people into my life who became good friends and colleagues. These associations created many serendipitous encounters. It is safe to say that these relationships significantly contributed to my success and wealth.

I have participated in triathlons to raise money for worthy causes; served Thanksgiving dinner at a homeless shelter; contributed to the Fairtax movement; and wrote checks to countless charities and foundations. In my home we never threw away anything that could be useful to others. We packaged it up and dropped it off at Goodwill or the Salvation Army. These contributions didn't make me a "good guy", they helped me become a better person and a well-rounded professional.

As with any endeavor one only gets out what one puts in, so it is important to not only join, but to contribute!

Data point

At What Age are Americans Most Likely to Volunteer?

% of Americans Who Volunteer By Age: 2014 Current Pupulatioin Survey Data

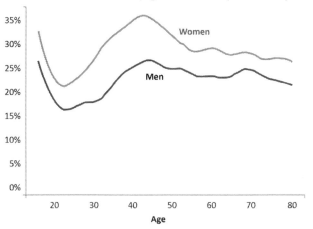

Source: United States Department of Commerce. Bureau of Census, United States Department of Labor.

Economic status is a key determinant of how likely a person is to volunteer. The sociologist and volunteerism researcher Hiromi Taniguchi writes that volunteering is "a privilege as well as a responsibility." People who find themselves in poverty or struggling to find a job are unlikely to feel that they can spend time and effort volunteering. People from a family with incomes of over $150,000 are more than twice as likely to volunteer than those from families with less than $50,000, and those who work full-time are nearly 20% more likely to volunteer than those who are unemployed.

Strategies and tips for joining and contributing to professional, community, charitable, and social orgs

 So how do you put this adaptive behavior into practice?

First, define your goals for joining. Is it to learn, network, obtain a certification, give back, or build your reputation? Perhaps all of the above, but prioritize. Think about what you need to get out of the association at this stage of your career. No need to overextend yourself. Only take on what you can comfortably squeeze into your schedule and then do it well.

Second, after joining, be super selective about what you volunteer to do. Be careful about getting roped into doing something that doesn't align with your reasons for joining to begin with. If you spend all your time stuffing envelopes and not meeting anyone or learning anything, it's a waste of time. Yes, I know, someone has to stuff envelopes; just not you. Never feel guilty about tactfully declining to do something which is not a good use of your time.

Third, become a "customer" of an influential member. Perhaps you decide to join the local Chamber of Commerce. Find one of the oldest, most influential members and "buy" something from them. Perhaps he or she sells cars, does business coaching, or accounting? When you become THEIR customer, they will look for ways to reciprocate and refer customers to you.

Fourth, establish charitable giving through a central conduit. Have you ever wondered why wealthy people set up a trust or foundation? It's because they would otherwise be overwhelmed by requests for donations from thousands of worthy causes. For example, you can give annually to the United Way, Red Cross, or a Charitable Giving Account. These conduits support many different causes. Whenever you are asked to give, you can honestly say, "I give via xyz every year". This doesn't preclude you from making ad hoc donations when you like, but it will give you an easy out when you need it. You can simply respond, "Have you applied for funding through my designated charitable giving organization?".

Fifth, be sensitive about championing certain political, religious, ethnic, cultural or social causes at work. It's great to be involved in causes you believe in, but it's important to remember your colleagues may not believe in them. In fact, they may believe in the exact opposite! I was once scolded by the president of a professional association for suggesting the association take a stand on climate change and the need for alternative energy. It's always a good idea to separate your professional life from your political, cultural, religious and social life. Not everyone has to believe what you believe, or see the world the same way, for you to have a mutually beneficial relationship with them.

Sixth, and this might seem a tad disingenuous, but it works: join an organization your boss or investors belong to, or volunteer or contribute to causes they believe in. Hey, many careers have been made by learning to play golf with the boss or joining her country club. Nothing endears one to one's heart quite like another who takes up one's causes. I have not been above joining the clubs my customers belonged to and have always found it to be both financially and socially rewarding.

Seventh, when you join any organization, latch on to the person who knows "where all the bodies are buried". There are always a few people who know the history, the personalities, the programs, and the drama that comprises every organization. You can save yourself a lot of time by knowing the people and things that matter and avoiding those that do not. Depending on the type of organization you join, find yourself a good mentor or sponsor to show you the ropes of the organization.

Finally, think about starting your own organization or a new chapter of an existing organization. There are a lot of needs and much left to do in any profession or community. Founding a worthwhile organization or chapter can give you tremendous credibility and clout. I have founded several chapters of both profit and nonprofit organizations. Doing so is not only good for the soul, it is good for business.

The Final Word, by Gretchen Rubin[12]

"Volunteering to help others is the right thing to do, and it also boosts personal happiness; a review of research by the Corporation for National and Community Service shows that those who aid the causes they value tend to be happier and in better health. They show fewer signs of physical and mental aging. And it's not just that helpful people also tend to be healthier and happier; helping others causes happiness."

Good reads and resources

The power of serendipity!
Lillian Eichler Watson,

Make a Difference: America's Guide to Volunteering and Community Service
by Arthur I. Blaustein

The Changemaker Ripple Effect: How One Person Can Transform the Lives of Thousands When Driven by Passion, Purpose and Boldness
by Sarah Boxx

Bowling Alone: The Collapse and Revival of American Community
by Robert D. Putnam

Happier at Home and The Happiness Project
by Gretchen Rubin

This Is Where You Belong: The Art and Science of Loving the Place You Live
by Melody Warnick

13. Choose domestic partners and best friends who make you a better person and a more effective professional.

The Chief Operating Officer of Facebook, Sheryl Sandberg, advised, *"When looking for a life partner, my advice to women is date all of them: the bad boys, the cool boys, the commitment-phobic boys, the crazy boys. But do not marry them. The things that make the bad boys sexy do not make them good husbands. When it comes time to settle down, find someone who wants an equal partner. Someone who thinks women should be smart, opinionated and ambitious. Someone who values fairness and expects or, even better, wants to do his share in the home. These men exist and, trust me, over time, nothing is sexier."*

The Australian Composer, Franz Schubert, said, "Happy is the man who finds a true friend, and far happier is he who finds that true friend in his wife." The poet, Adam Lindsay Gordon, wrote some of my favorite words:

"There comes a point in your life when you realize:
Who matters,
Who never did,
Who won't anymore,
And who always will.
So, don't worry about people from your past, there's a reason why they didn't make it to your future."

You may be wondering what choosing a spouse, life partner, or best friend has to do with professionalism. My first boss and mentor, Durward Owen, would say: "EVERYTHING". It is one of the most important decisions you will make in your life and it can make or break your career. Durward taught me: your life partner and closest companions will do one of three things for you:

1) nothing,
2) hold you back, or
3) improve you.

True professionals choose well....and if they find after due time that those choices resulted in number 1 or 2, they have the courage to do a "reset" and choose again. Find the right life partner or best friend behind door number 3.

Note: You may have more than one life partner over the course of your professional career, many people do. You will likely have more than one best friend. Your best friend, by the way, can be a parent, sibling or other relative. You may have multiple business partners who are also close friends. Used herein, the word "partner(s)" means one or more life partners, best friends or close business partners. It means the one or two people you are (or will be) the closest to upon commencing your partnership.

What does it mean to choose domestic partners and best friends who make you a better person and a more effective professional?

As a true professional you realize your partners are the closest and best "connections" you will have in your life for an indefinite period of time; perhaps your entire lifetime. They will influence your thinking, moods, ambition, drive and determination. Your fates are intertwined. If you are unhappy at home, you will be unhappy and unproductive at work. Your home and your off time are your sanctuaries. If you are always fighting battles there you cannot effectively fight the battles at work.

You see your long-term partners as confidants and sounding boards. You are not afraid to share your deepest hopes and fears with them. They are perhaps the only ones whom you are not afraid of being vulnerable. You value their opinions and perspectives. They may or may not be directly involved in your profession, but they know you better than anyone else and what you are trying to accomplish. They push you when you need to be pushed, and pull you up or along when you need to be pulled. And, of course, you do the same for them.

A true example

Whenever someone asked my first boss, Durward Owen, what he attributed most to his success, he would always reply, "I married up." Everyone who knew his wife, Connie, would nod their heads in agreement. She was definitely his "better half". In his teachings, Durward would emphasize "marrying up" does not mean marrying someone wealthier, or with better breeding than yourself (although he was quick to add that doesn't hurt). He taught the importance of choosing a life partner who would support and compliment your professional endeavors. This advice stuck with me through my dating and courting years.

I married Jill in 1987 after a one year courtship. She often recounted later how she felt as if she was interviewing for a job. After winning the internship (getting engaged), she was on probation to prove she was deserving of the full-time job (marriage). In all fairness to myself, I was a bit more romantic than that: I just wanted to make sure her life goals and aspirations were aligned with mine. Durward had always taught me never to subjugate your goals or happiness to someone else's.

Jill and I were partners in every sense of the word for nearly 25 years. We raised three kids, built a nice home, and helped each other with our respective careers. She often accompanied me on business trips and would work the booth at trade shows, charming customers and taking orders for the products. The entrepreneurial lifestyle can be stressful and fraught with risk. Jill would often worry, but she was always a trooper and always supported my dreams no matter how tough things got, and they got very tough at times. Later in our marriage she wanted to run her own business, so I helped her start and build a hair salon.

As an aspiring entrepreneur, I was doubly blessed because one of my best friends, Gary, helped me to launch my second company. From both a personal and professional perspective he was a dream partner. Gary had financial acumen and operational skills I did not have at the time. He was thoughtful and even tempered; able to smooth out the extreme highs and lows of building a business at the frantic pace required in the high-tech industry. Jill was my better half at home. Gary was my better half at work. Without them I never would have become as successful as I did.

Jill and I divorced in 2012. Quite simply, the marriage wasn't working any longer from either a personal or professional perspective. Our respective goals for what we wanted for the rest of our lives were no longer aligned. There is no use faking it, or going through the motions. Durward also taught "life is too short". We parted ways but remain good friends to this day. Gary married, had four kids, and went his separate way after we sold the company. He had a very successful career in his own right. We don't see each other as much, but we stay in touch.

This story is an important lesson of life and professional success. As I said earlier in this chapter, people will come and go in and out of your life. Not every relationship will last forever, but you must pick and choose your closest partners very carefully.

Today I am fortunate to have another life partner. She is an absolutely incredible person. I know for certain Durward would say, "She's definitely your better half." Perhaps you will meet her a little later in this book.

Data point

Divorced, Separated, or in Second or Later Marriage

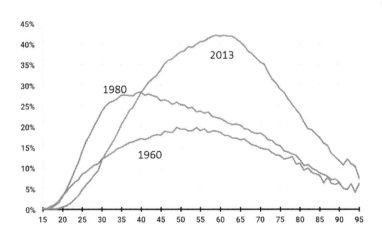

Source: Census Data

It's no secret that about 50% of marriages end in divorce. When you break that down by number of marriages, about 41 percent of first marriages end in divorce; 60 percent of second marriages end in divorce; and 73 percent of third marriages end in divorce. The divorce rate is the highest during a couple's peak income-producing years. A divorce can have a significant financial and emotional impact on an upwardly-mobile professional. One of the most important things true professionals do is to choose their partners wisely and to keep their marriages together.

Strategies and tips for choosing life partners and best friends who make you a better person and a more effective professional.

 So how do you put this adaptive behavior into practice?

First, choose partners with whom you believe there is mutual trust, respect, loyalty, and shared values. It's important to share your mutual aspirations and expectations *early* in the relationship. You may not yet know exactly what you want to do for a living, but your partner needs to have a sense of your direction and how big your dreams and goals are. If it's a spouse, discuss the conditions under which either of you will sacrifice your career if you need to relocate. It's important to lay the ground work for work-life balance, such as working late, working at home, or spending a lot of time away from home because of travel and other work commitments.

Second, choose partners who are lifelong learners, who want to keep growing. If they expect you to be "finished" or you expect it of them, you are both in trouble. Choose partners who see you as an unfinished masterpiece; a constant work-in-progress. They believe in your full potential and you believe equally in theirs.

Third, choose partners who know a little something about your profession, or are willing to learn. Few things will be more impressive to your colleagues than a partner who can converse intelligently about the business you are involved in when they meet your partners at social events. It's a real bonus if your partners know your colleagues by name, and their life partner's names, as well as their role and accomplishments.

Fourth, take a personality assessment test with your partners, or go on a personal development retreat every few years. There are a variety of wonderful tools and events designed to help partners better understand each other and grow together. People do change. You will change. Your partners will change. Work with your partners to change and improve together.

Fifth, develop a secret language or agree on discreet visual or verbal cues to use with your partners in social and professional settings. Your partners might use these cues to signal you to hush up, calm down, or slow down on the drinking. You might use these cues to signal to your partners it is time to make a graceful exit. Good partners can almost read each other's minds, but when they can't, it's helpful to give and receive secret cues. After all, you're a team!

Sixth, regroup and set goals at least annually to make sure you are still on the same page; still want the same things. When I was married to Jill, we sat down for one whole day each year and talked about what we wanted to do in the coming year. We agreed upon and wrote down our goals, both personally and professionally. Nothing was off the table. We talked about budget, vacations, housing, college funds, friends to jettison and new friends we wanted to make. These domestic things always needed to be aligned with our respective professional demands and limitations.

Seventh, learn to back off and let each other go from time to time. The best partners need a break from one another on occasion. A healthy separation can spur renewed commitment, or perhaps the realization the partnership is spent. If after an appropriate break you are not dying to see each other again and pick up the charge for your respective challenges ahead, for heaven's sake don't bury it or ignore it too long. Your life will suffer. Your professional aspirations may start to wane. Drifting aimlessly in a dead-end partnership leaves you with what's behind door number 1 or 2: nothing, or a relationship that holds you back.

Finally, to maintain a strong sense of shared purpose, celebrate often! Your successes are your partners' successes, and vice versa. When one of you gets a promotion, you both rise and benefit. When one of you gets a new opportunity, you both stretch and grow. From a purely professional perspective, you both get to be on two journeys and lead two simultaneous lives. Most people don't even live one life well. You and your partners are living at least two re-markable lives.

The Final Word, by Ashton Kutcher[13]

> "I really think that you have to find a partner that compliments you and is somebody that pushes you and is better at some things than you are, so they can push you to improve yourself as a person."

Good reads and resources

Marry Wisely, Marry Well
by Ernie Baker

Trophy Man: The Surprising Secrets of Black Women Who Marry Well
by Dr. Joy McElroy

Designing Your Life: How to Build a Well-Lived, Joyful Life
by Bill Burnett and Dave Evans

Best Friends Forever
by Kimberla Lawson Roby

Finding the Love Of Your Life
by Neil Clark Warren

Finding Your Life Partner
by Jess Rodgers

You & Your Partner, Inc.
by Jeffrey McIntyre and Miriam Hawley

14. Associate with positive, forward thinking doers; avoid chronic complainers and naysayers.

The acclaimed actress and singer Selena Gomez, advised, *"You are who you surround yourself with. I know that's such a cliché quote, but it's true."*

Accomplished people are selective about whom they associate with. They surround themselves with people who lift them up and challenge them in constructive ways. Many will tell you their success was due in part because they hired or partnered with people who were smarter and more talented than themselves. Whatever it is they need done that truly matters, they actively track down the best people they can find at doing it and associate themselves with those people.

Conversely, accomplished people learn how to expunge or neutralize chronic complainers and naysayers. They learned early in their careers that perpetual negativity and bad attitudes are toxic. No matter how important or protected a toxic person may be, true professionals develop strategies for marginalizing those people's control and influence over them, even if it means transferring or changing jobs. The true professional does not try to win over or change toxic people because that is a lost cause. They ignore or avoid them and look for ways to go around them.

What does it mean to associate with positive, forward thinking doers, and avoid chronic complainers and naysayers?

As a true professional you seek out the people who are making things happen. You develop a can-do attitude because you only associate with can-do people. You learn to recognize the positive deviants in your profession and learn from their innate ability to solve problems and move forward. You value thoughtfulness and authenticity. You shun obnoxious know-it-alls and people who are vexatious to your spirit. You seek to surround yourself with positive energy and shield yourself from negative energy. Your mind can only hold one of three thoughts at any one time: positive, negative or neutral. You work at entertaining mostly positive thoughts.

You do not confuse constructive confrontation, respectful disagreement and debate, with negativity. Just because someone disagrees with you does not make them a naysayer. In fact, you feed off healthy debate and disagreement with determined and positive people, because they force you to get better...smarter. It is not so much what they say that you admire, it is what they do when all is said and done. You are not attracted to people who enjoy arguing for the sake of arguing. You are attracted to people who brainstorm, research, think, analyze, converse, debate, and decide with an unrelenting determination to get things done.

Most importantly, you seek out and pattern yourself after good mentors and role models.

A true example

Darren was a perpetual pessimist. Ironically, he was a copywriter in the small advertising agency I worked for. It always struck me as odd how one who largely viewed people and the world with cynicism could write advertisements to convince people to buy our client's products. In our staff meeting every Monday he was always quick to say why this campaign would not work and why that idea was a bad one. The owner of the ad agency, Ken, had a bit of a pessimistic streak himself. I think he enjoyed having Darren around because he made Ken look like a progressive, forward-thinking optimist in comparison.

I was only a few years into my career and didn't have much practical advertising or marketing experience. My job was to find new clients for the agency and to perform billable work as a relationship manager on the accounts I brought in. About six months into the job I realized many local businesses we were trying to attract as clients thought of our agency as stodgy and old-school. The newer agencies in town had younger, more hip, and more seemingly creative talent.

One day I was reading an article in the local newspaper about a talk the governor of the state had given on economic development. He was quoted as saying the biggest problem with most companies in our state was they were lousy marketers. Despite being great manufacturers, he said, our companies lacked marketing know-how. That seemed to me to be a great opportunity to reposition our advertising agency as a full-service advertising AND "marketing" agency. I called the state economic development office and offered to conduct marketing workshops in every major city in the state if they would sponsor them, help promote them, and cover the expenses. To my surprise and delight, they agreed.

Upon pitching the opportunity at our weekly staff meeting, Darren immediately went on a rant about what a bad idea it was. He claimed it would distract the agency from billable work. "Besides," he said, "Mike doesn't know anything about marketing. He'll just make us look stupid." Ken, however, was no fool. He saw it as an opportunity to get his agency in front of hundreds of new prospective clients throughout the entire state. He gave me the green light to develop the workshop and organize the road show.

To develop the workshop and the workbook I bought and devoured every book on marketing I could get my hands on. I watched videos of seminars given by marketing experts in other states. I called the heads of marketing at the most successful companies in the region and asked them for their three biggest lessons for effective marketing. In short, I became a marketing "expert" in short order. Although I was not yet street smart, I was definitely book smart.

Darren's job was to help me write and edit the copy for the workbook. He was also supposed to develop the copy for the promotional materials the state economic development office was going to send to every business in the state inviting them to the workshop. He dragged his feet, complained incessantly, and did whatever he could to sabotage me and the project. Having no choice, and this is weird, I sought out a friend who was a copywriter and editor at a competing ad agency and asked him for help. He was happy to oblige. He loved the project and worked on it in his spare time. He got other creative talent to contribute as well. I delivered the raw material, minus all of Darren's input, to our creative staff to design and produce the book and promo materials. Darren, of course, was livid I had gone around him.

The workshops were a smash hit. They were held in nine different cities over nine consecutive days. Every one of them was sold out, standing room only. People who had missed it in one city drove across the entire state to catch it in another city because they heard it was so good. The workshop made front page news in the business section of the local newspapers in every city where it was held. I had recruited a variety of experts to speak in each city, but I was the main facilitator. My reputation soared. The ad agency picked up several new clients around the state.

Darren made a big stand at our staff meeting following the marketing workshop road show. He told Ken, "Either Mike goes or I go!" He was fired on the spot. In short, Darren was a naysayer and generally toxic person. When you run into the Darrens in your career, never let them drag you down. Work around them.

Data point

Source: The Five Dysfunctions of a Team, Patrick Lencioni

In his best-selling book, The Five Dysfunctions of a Team, Patrick Lencioni explores the fundamental causes of organizational politics and team failure. It's a worthy read. Even teams comprised of positive, forward-looking doers, can falter. However, it's a foregone conclusion that teams comprised of chronic complainers and naysayers, i.e., toxic people, have no chance of success.

Strategies and tips for associating with positive, forward-thinking doers, and avoiding chronic complainers and naysayers

 So how do you put this adaptive behavior into practice?

First, in any organization you join, figure out who the top one third are. The top one third are those who consistently do two thirds of the work. Those are the people to associate with. The middle one third do their fair share; one third of the work. They are neither positive or negative, but they are not particularly good to hang out with lest you become one of them and fall into the habit of doing only what you need to do to get by. The bottom one third do little, if anything, and are probably a drag on the organization. They are the ones to avoid and work around.

Second, listen carefully to what your associates say about others who are not present. If they gossip about them or tear them down they will likely do the same to you behind your back. Gravitate to associates who speak well of others and who, if they have something negative to say about someone, it is truthful about their actions or behaviors and not about them personally.

Third, associate with people who accept you for who you are and don't think they have to make you into something you are not. They listen to and respect your opinions, even if they don't agree with them. Be wary of people who are immediately dismissive, whether it be of others or an idea. Dismissive people have closed minds. You will never learn anything from them.

Fourth, surround yourself with people who have goals and plans and are taking tangible steps towards achieving them. Many people talk about what they plan to do but few actually work towards it. There is a popular urban saying, "Money talks, bullsh*t walks". You have to pay to play. You have to be willing to invest time, money and energy into any endeavor. Associate with those who "walk the walk, not just talk the talk".

Fifth, avoid people who live in the past. People who are always talking about how great things used to be and how the world is now going to hell in a handbasket are emotionally and intellectually trapped in a bygone era. You learn from the past, but you live in the present in a way that creates a better future. How you think about your future determines its outcome. If you associate with people who think the future will be bleak, that is the way your future will turn out.

Sixth, associate with people who are fast to forgive. People who hold a grudge and take forever to get over something that turned out badly, or someone who did them wrong, are emotionally retarded. Sh*t happens; get over it. Positive, forward-thinking doers learn to forgive and let go. Surround yourself with people who do something about a slight or wrong if there is something constructive which can be done, and who learn from it and move on when it is irreconcilable.

Seventh, seek out natural collaborators who are willing to share their knowledge, experience and positive energy. Magic happens when people work constructively together. It's more than "two brains are better than one". The collective energy of two or more people working towards a positive, common purpose enables you to tap into the energy of the universe and the wisdom of the ages. This phenomenon isn't mystic fantasy; it is rooted in scientific theory.

Finally, benefiting fully from positive associations requires you to do three things: 1) Give and take feedback, 2) Trust, and 3) Empathize. It is very hard to take constructive feedback from people you do not trust. It is impossible to give constructive feedback if you do not empathize with the people whom you are giving it to. Strive to truly understand your associates. We are all complex human beings. The only way to break through the tangled complexities of human knowledge, emotion and experiences, is to "feel" people, not merely see and hear them. In this sense, this behavior does not just lead to positive associations, it leads to more meaningful relationships.

The Final Word, by Colin Powell[14]

"The less you associate with some people, the more your life will improve. Any time you tolerate mediocrity in others, it increases your mediocrity. An important attribute in successful people is their impatience with negative thinking and negative acting people. Friends that don't help you climb will want you to crawl. Your friends will stretch your vision or choke your dream. Those that don't increase you will eventually decrease you."

Good reads and resources

Emotional Vampires at Work: Dealing with Bosses and Coworkers Who Drain You Dry
by Albert Bernstein

Safe People: How to Find Relationships That Are Good for You and Avoid Those That Aren't
by Henry Cloud and John Townsend

The Charisma Myth: How Anyone Can Master the Art and Science of Personal Magnetism
by Olivia Fox Cabane

Coping with Difficult People: The Proven-Effective Battle Plan That Has Helped Millions Deal with the Troublemakers in Their Lives at Home and at Work
by Robert M. Bramson

Who's Pushing Your Buttons?: Handling the Difficult People in Your Life
by John Townsend

How Successful People Think: Change Your Thinking, Change Your Life
by John C. Maxwell

The Five Dysfunctions of a Team
by Patrick Lencioni

15. Give people your full attention when engaging with them.

The American scholar and public speaker, Brene Brown, said, "I define connection as the energy that exists between people when they feel seen, heard, and valued; when they can give and receive without judgment; and when they derive sustenance and strength from the relationship."

True professionals make others feel heard and appreciated. They don't rush the conversation. They listen more than they talk. They prescribe to the old saying, "Talk is cheap because supply exceeds demand." When you are in their presence, you feel special: the way they look at you, smile, nod thoughtfully in response to your points, and express themselves in their reply.

True professionals train themselves to engage with others in a positive and authentic manner. Their body language is open and receptive. They have a strong gravitational pull; it's hard not to be sucked in by their gravitas towards you. The truly great ones can warp time when you are with them. An hour of conversation seems like only a few minutes. You wonder where the time went.

What does it mean to give people your full attention when engaging with them?

As a true professional you look people in the eyes and give them your undivided attention. You don't merely feign interest in what they are saying as you scan your mobile phone or look around the room to see who else is present. You focus your full attention on the person you are engaging with.

When in a conversation with several people your eyes and your body shift casually between each one as they speak. You consciously avoid folding your arms, frowning, or using body language or facial expressions that may communicate to others you are either disinterested in what they are saying or disagree with it.

When engaging in meaningful conversation with others you have trained your mind from racing forward too fast. You have the discipline to remain focused on what they are saying rather than thinking about what to say in reply. You have trained yourself to withhold judgment and expressing an opinion until all others in the conversation have expressed their initial opinions.

If you are pressed for time, or have a lot on your mind that is distracting you from fully engaging, you apologize and beg their forgiveness. You reassure them their issues are important to you. You promise them you will take up the conversation again when you are not rushed and in a better frame of mind.

A true example.

Upon selling my second company I went to work for the acquiring company as part of the terms of the deal. I reported to Jeremy, the Vice President of Marketing and Sales. By all outward appearances, Jeremy was an impressive professional. He was always impeccably dressed. He had a law degree and an MBA degree. He had worked as an executive for a successful Silicon Valley tech company and had deep knowledge of the industry. He had a strong work ethic and was thought by everyone in the company to be dedicated and loyal. Jeremy, however, suffered from a fatal character flaw that derailed his career on multiple occasions. He loved to hear himself talk.

Jeremy always did his homework and showed up well prepared for every meeting. No doubt he thought this behavior gave him license to dominate the conversation. Whenever anyone else spoke up, Jeremy had a bad habit of interrupting them and talking over them. He would mumble, "Ah uh, h'mmm, yep, yep, ah uh, okay, okay…" He wasn't intentionally trying to be rude. He was very smart and his brain could absorb information very quickly. But he gave people the impression he was disinterested in what they had to say and simply wanted them to finish quickly so he could retake the floor.

A few months after I joined the company Jeremy was fired. The company was publicly traded and had reported lower than expected quarterly sales. Wall

Street punished the stock. It wasn't all Jeremy's fault, but he made a convenient fall guy. I helped him pack his office, load his car with boxes, and watched him drive away with tears in his eyes.

Two years later Jeremy called me about a job opening at his new company. I interviewed with the executive team and accepted the job. I was particularly impressed with Kyle, the Founder and CEO. He was warm, thoughtful, and highly engaging. He looked people in the eye and let them talk as long as they had something useful to say. He often encouraged people to take over the white board and lead an impromptu brainstorming session. He wrote a personal note on the paychecks of every employee every two weeks, noting what they had done for the company during that pay period and thanking them for their valuable contribution. He was one of the most thoughtful and engaging leaders I had ever met. I later patterned myself on his example when running my own company again.

Jeremy, on the other hand, had not changed a bit. The employees at Kyle's company joked about how Jeremy liked to "hold court". In one exchange with a nationally renowned branding expert who was hired to help design the name and packaging for our new software product, Jeremy presented his idea for a premier edition of the product. The package would be separate from the package which would be sold through retail channels. As the branding expert attempted to explain why that was an ill-advised strategy, Jeremy sat in his chair, looked down at his shoes, and mumbled, "Ah uh, h'mmm, yep, yep, ah uh, okay, okay..." He then proceeded to ignore the expert's advice and create a premier edition of the product.

The premier edition of the product was very expensive, generated no revenue, and created no favorable publicity. It was a total flop. The shareholders thought it was a waste of money. Jeremy was fired. I helped him pack his office, load his car with boxes, and watched him drive away with tears in his eyes.

One year later I launched my third company. Jeremy walked through the door and convinced me to hire him as Vice President of Business Development.

Against my better judgment, I gave him the job. I figured he had learned his lesson and everyone deserves redemption. In practice, he had not changed much. He still had the bad habit of interrupting people and talking over them in meetings. A year later, I stepped aside as CEO to make way for Bernice, a new CEO the board wanted to bring in because she had experience with bringing tech companies public.

In an irony of ironies, Bernice turned out to have the same disconcerting habit as Jeremy. She did emails during staff meetings, rarely looking up to engage with the executives making their weekly reports. She took personal phone calls during board meetings, making us all wait until she finished. After all, it was her meeting. She constantly interrupted people and talked over them whenever it suited her. One of the first things she did as the new CEO was to fire Jeremy. A year later, the board fired her.

The common thread between Jeremy, Kyle and Bernice was the way they engaged with people. Jeremy and Bernice gave people the impression they cared little for what they had to say. They rarely gave people their full attention. Both of their careers were beset with a series of firings and failures.

Kyle successfully sold his company to Microsoft and had a long and distinguished career there. His example taught me to "shut up" after making my point and concentrate fully on what people were saying and how they were saying it. I contribute this learned behavior to helping me win over employees, investors, partners, and clients. My better half would also confirm it helped me to win her over as well!

Data point

3 most important things to people in a conversation

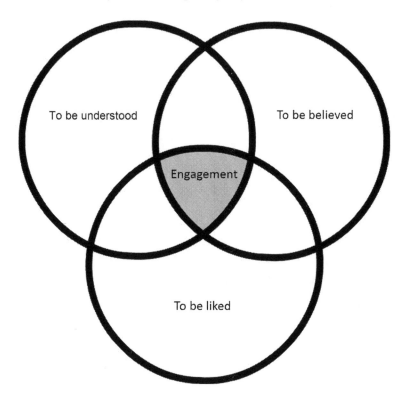

You don't have to be a social scientist to know what factors determine people's level of engagement when conversing with others. You know this from how engaged you feel when conversing with someone, whether it be for work or social purposes. You want to be heard and understood. You want to be taken seriously. And you want to be liked and valued. Don't we all? Practice these three engagement techniques when interacting with others and people will always view you as a true professional.

Strategies and tips for giving people your full attention when engaging with them.

 So how do you put this internalized behavior into practice?

First, use the name of the person you are conversing with in the conversation. There is nothing sweeter to people than the sound of their own name. When being introduced to someone for the first time, use a memory trick to imprint their name on your brain. Use their name during the conversation, or at the end. Say, "John, it was great to meet you. I hope we get a chance to talk again."

Second, avoid gratuitous name dropping. Throwing out the names of important people you know may come across as grandstanding. It's fine to recite a name in the context of the conversation, especially when offering to introduce that person to the one you are conversing with, but dropping names out of context can come across as a superficial attempt to impress people. People are less impressed with who you know and more impressed by how you engage with them and listening carefully to what they are saying.

Third, avoid one-upmanship. When a coworker is telling you about his or her vacation, don't throw in how much more exotic your vacation was. If someone tells you about the 5K they just ran, don't tell them about the full marathon you ran last year, unless they ask you about it. You know these kind of people, always having to one-up everyone else. They come across as shallow and insecure. Don't be one of those people!

Fourth, pause before responding. There is power in silence. After someone makes their point, don't jump right in to respond. Wait a few seconds, collect your thoughts, and then proceed in a thoughtful manner. This simple technique sends a signal to people you not only heard what they said, you are thinking about it before you comment on it. In the words of the Roman philosopher, Marcus Tullius Ciero, "Silence is one of the great arts of conversation."

Fifth, parrot back or clarify what someone just told you before responding. One of my former partners had a great technique. After an explanation by someone in the room, he would say, "Let me repeat what I think you just said." He would then summarize it and ask if that was right. Often the person would clarify because they realize they did not make their point as clear as it could have been. Once there was full agreement on what was said, my partner would proceed to address it. My partner heeded the advice of The Dalai Lama: "When you talk, you are only repeating what you already know. But if you listen, you may learn something new."

Sixth, if someone is rambling on or saying something you know to be untrue or off base, interrupt them politely. You can say in a respectful way, "Wait, timeout; this conversation is off topic (or getting out of hand)." You can say, "I'm sorry, I believe you believe it, but let me say what I know to be a fact." Separate fact from opinion in the conversation. If it's opinion, you can agree to disagree when everyone has been heard. And for heaven's sake, don't ever talk over people. Don't be a Jeremy!

Seventh, look people in the eyes when you talk to them and give them your full attention. I know I already said that, but it bears repeating over and over until it becomes internalized. If you get a text or phone call, or someone waves to you from across the room, say, "Excuse me, I have to take this or say hi to someone." To be on your phone or looking all around the room to see who else is there sends a signal to the people you are speaking with that you are more important than they are and don't value their presence.

Finally, play a mental game with yourself during every conversation with coworkers and colleagues. Try to learn something new about them, or elicit from them a fact or story you did not know before the conversation. Make this a goal: you are not permitted to leave the conversation until you have achieved it. At the end of the conversation you can say something like, "Well, I learned something new today. I didn't know xyz." This always impresses people. They feel good by having taught or shared something you value. As a bonus, follow up with a text or email to thank them for the conversation, or to let them know how you will follow up on it.

The Final Word, by Ann Voskamp[15]

"When I fully enter time's swift current, enter into the current moment with the weight of all my attention, I slow the torrent with the weight of me all here."

Good reads and resources

The Charisma Myth: How Anyone Can Master the Art and Science of Personal Magnetism
by Olivia Fox Cabane

Understanding Social Psychology Across Cultures: Engaging with Others in a Changing World
by Peter K Smith and Ronald Fischer

Reclaiming Conversation: The Power of Talk in a Digital Age
by Sherry Turkle

Quiet: The Power of Introverts in a World That Can't Stop Talking
by Susan Cain

Crucial Conversations: Tools for Talking When Stakes Are High
by Kerry Patterson and Joseph Grenny

The 5 Love Languages
by Gary Chapman

What Every BODY is Saying: An Ex-FBI Agent's Guide to Speed-Reading People
by Joe Navarro and Marvin Karlins

CHAPTER 4

AWARE

This is the PERSONAL you, how you stay <u>thoughtful</u> and authentic.

It's about truthfulness, temperament, weaknesses and blind spots, mindfulness, and challenge.

16. Tell the truth and keep your word.

The Hindu spiritual teacher Sivananda Saraswati, taught, "You should always keep your word. All the setbacks in life come only because you don't keep your word."

Regardless of their wealth or stature, the most admired people have a reputation for integrity. They tell the truth and keep their word. In their personal and professional lives they have a strong moral center. No amount of money, no job or accomplishment, is worth it to them if it involves abandoning these core principles. No contract is needed when doing business with them. Their word is their bond. This one behavior, above all others, is often cited by their colleagues and associates as the reason they are held in such high regard as true professionals.

What does it mean to tell the truth and keep your word?

As a true professional, your integrity is not for sale. It is as important to you as oxygen, because you are fully aware your professional life depends upon it. You don't delude yourself into believing you can compromise your integrity occasionally. You don't rationalize lying or going back on your word as a necessary evil.

You subscribe to the philosophy you never have to remember what you said to whom, because what you say is always what you believe to be the truth, and you intend to stand by it. You are aware a lie never dies. You never have to worry about being held accountable for what you say or promise. You say what you are going to do and you do what you say.

A true example

After leaving my first job under the tutelage of Durward Owen, I ventured into the "real world" where I did not have the advantages of the same examples and protections I enjoyed while working for Durward. I learned quickly the business world is full of charlatans. Deceit and half-truths were the rule of the day. The road to success was to over-promise and under-deliver. Tell people whatever they wanted to hear to get the order.

It was a jarring, eye-opening adjustment. Many of those whom I saw succeeding were bold faced liars and disingenuous glad-handlers. They rarely kept their word. I began to think, "If you can't beat them, join them." I wanted wealth and success and I was determined to do whatever it took to achieve both.

My new role model was Marty, an ambitious, charming, fast-talking entrepreneur who was starting a new high-tech venture. I was thrilled to be invited to be his cofounder. I learned soon enough Marty had a loose association with the truth. When we were pitching investors, half of what he said I knew to be a lie. I couldn't contradict him, so I mimicked him. Our favorite line was, "Yes, our technology does that." We routinely promised capabilities we did not have and deadlines we could not meet.

Marty's philosophy was, "we eat what we kill" and "kill or be killed". He was the opposite of Durward Owen in every respect. Durward lived and worked in the relatively safe nonprofit world. Marty lived and worked in the ruthless and unforgiving, for-profit world. I figured I was now in the real world: this was how business was done. I thought I needed to adapt or die. I didn't want my business career to be over before it started. This, of course, was a convenient rationalization for unethical behavior. It's the thinking of a person who is not self-aware. It's how many careers get off to the wrong start.

Marty and I raised $3M for our new company. It was a lot of money in those days and a heady accomplishment for a young man of 25 years of age. Half-truths and over-promising, telling investors and customers whatever they wanted to hear, became a daily habit. It was working. It was the path to great success...at least in my impressionable young mind.

Our investors were not as naïve as we would have liked. They suspected we needed "adult supervision" and forced us to merge with another one of their investments, another high-tech company run by two seasoned professionals.

Both were also former Navy fighter pilots. They had a different code of ethics and quickly caught on to our game plan. They started holding us accountable. Marty, of course, in his typical kill-or-be-killed mindset, deflected most of the blame onto me. His role in the company was slowly marginalized. I was summarily fired.

Getting fired from a company I helped to start was a wakeup call. Directionless, I fell back on someone I could trust and get guidance from: Durward Owen. He hired me back and sent me far away, to the heartland of America. He knew I needed a new environment and a fresh start. Thus began my redemption and a complete reset as an aspiring professional.

Data point

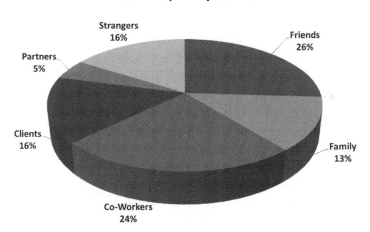

Most Frequently Lied To

Strangers 16%

Friends 26%

Partners 5%

Clients 16%

Family 13%

Co-Workers 24%

Source: Robert Feldman, Professor of Psychology at the University of Massachusetts, Liar: The Truth About Lying

Lying is a common human behavior. Just about everyone does it in some form. Most lies are harmless, as in "white lies" told to avoid hurting someone's feelings. Perhaps it is because lying is so common that many people say they value honesty above almost every other human quality. It may surprise you to learn that people lie to their bosses and co-workers more than just about every other group of people in their lives – even more than strangers. Such behavior, if it becomes a habit, can have catastrophic effects that can kill a career and be difficult to recover from.

Strategies and tips for telling the truth and keeping your word

 So how do you put this internalized behavior into practice?

First, consider your word to be both a promise and a commitment. When you assure a person you will do something, you don't quickly forget it. You remain dedicated to the purpose. See your reputation as the sum total of the promises and commitments you keep. Be the person you always want to do business with.

Second, avoid the tendency to trivialize the small, seemingly unimportant things you tell people because you know they will either forget, or not hold you accountable to them. Saying "I'll give you a call" or "we need to grab lunch" when you have no intention of doing so, is a bad habit to get into. Lots of small, trivial lies and half-truths, eventually add up to impugn your reputation.

Third, make fewer commitments and track the ones you do make. Put them on your calendar or make a note in your phone. *Follow up, follow through, and only agree to what you can do.* If you get a lot of requests, don't be so quick to agree, even if you want to do them or intend to do them. The road to ruin is paved with good intentions. Get in the habit of saying, "I would love to, but I can't make any promises. I don't want to commit to something I might not be able to deliver."

Fourth, make your word conditional on the word or action of whomever you are giving it to. For example, if a colleague says to you, "Will you send me your notes of the meeting I missed?" or "Can we schedule some time to talk about the project?". You can reply, "Sure, please send me an email reminder." or "No problem, send me a calendar invite with the objectives and agenda." Put the onus back on them to follow through first.

Fifth, call out contradictions and own up to miscues. Stay vigilant about what you say versus what your peers, colleagues, partners, subordinates and superiors say. If you say something that turns out to be untrue, or you are unable to keep your word based on the actions or inactions of others, own up to it. Get ahead of it by acknowledging the contradiction or miscue. Avoid the temptation to blame it on others. You can say, "I did not know that was untrue, but it is no excuse." or "I am sorry we failed to deliver as I promised. I had every reason to believe we could honor our commitments and I will do my best to correct the situation." People will usually quickly forgive if you own up to it.

Sixth, refuse to lie or overtly deceive if directed to do so by others. No job or relationship is worth it. No investment is sacred enough. Once you become culpable, your integrity and reputation are at stake. You could end up being the fall guy. It happens in corporate life every day. You don't necessarily have to be a whistleblower; you just want to avoid playing an active role in lies or cover ups. There is always another job, relationship, or investor, but you only have ONE reputation.

Seventh, refuse to associate with those who routinely lie, deceive, or fail to honor their word. Avoid guilt by association. You may have to work with them, or even report to them over the course of your career, but you do not have to associate with them. Heed the old saying, "When you lie down with dogs, you get fleas." Keep your distance and reject their attempts to associate with you. Dishonest people get their legitimacy and credibility by trying to associate with honest and legitimate people. If you must, make it clear to others that although you must work with an unscrupulous person, you do not agree with their behavior, nor do you practice their ways of doing business.

Finally, don't hesitate to subtlety remind people of how you have kept your commitments to them, and thank them for keeping their commitments to you. Most people will always take you for your word, unless you prove you are not good for it, but it does not hurt to remind them that you did what you said you would do. It's a subtle reminder to your associates you can consistently be trusted. Likewise, you should acknowledge others when they keep their word to you, or call them on it when they do not.

The Final Word, by Werner Erhard[16]

"Oversimplifying somewhat, honoring your word as we define it means you either keep your word (do what you said you would do and by the time you said you would do it), or as soon as you know that you will not, you say that you will not to those who were counting on your word and clean up any mess caused by not keeping your word."

Good reads and resources

The Four Agreements: A Practical Guide to Personal Freedom
by Don Miguel Ruiz and Janet Mills

Liar: The Truth About Lying
by Robert Feldman

Present Over Perfect: Leaving Behind Frantic for a Simpler, More Soulful Way of Living
by Shauna Niequist

Radical Honesty: How to Transform Your Life by Telling the Truth
by Brad Blanton and Marilyn Ferguson

Unglued: Making Wise Choices in the Midst of Raw Emotions
by Lysa TerKeurst

Business and Society: Ethics, Sustainability, and Stakeholder Management
by Archie B. Carroll and Ann K. Buchholtz

17. Manage your temperament; admit when you are wrong and apologize.

One of the foremost experts on temperament, the American psychologist, David Keirsey, concluded, *"Our brain is a sort of computer which has temperament for its hardware and character for its software."*

Many accomplished people have reputations for being demanding and difficult to work with. The most admired, and perhaps the ones others want to associate with the most, learn how to manage their temperaments. They have a reputation for being even tempered. They don't allow anger, anxiety, or frustration to get the better of them. They keep things in perspective.

True professionals believe people are not defined by what problems or challenges they are confronted with, but by how they choose to respond to them. Taking a cue from Keirsey's study and observations, true professionals learn how to control and "program" their temperaments, particularly when in the company of their associates. They don't let their pride get the best of them. They check their egos. They can admit when they are wrong and quickly apologize when corrected. They don't make excuses for their mistakes, they own up to them. They heed the wise words of Benjamin Franklin: "Never ruin an apology with an excuse."

What does it mean to manage your temperament; admit when you are wrong and apologize?

As a true professional, you are in command of your temperament and behavioral dispositions. They are not in command of you. You manage your mood swings. You are the master of your emotions. You are not quick to anger. You don't easily lose control, pout, cry, or throw fits in the presence of others. As incompetent, frustrating and infuriating as others may be, especially at work, you do not let them get the better of you. This does not mean you suffer fools easily. It means you don't allow them to break your character. You practice the behavior you want others to follow.

When you are wrong, as are the most well informed people from time to time, you graciously admit it and apologize if an apology is appropriate. When you do have a relapse in character, lash out, or treat others unfairly or with disrespect, you apologize for your behavior and pledge to be better. You are wise enough to heed the proverb, "Pride Go'eth Before the Fall". You are never too proud to utter three of the most important words in any relationship: "I am sorry."

A true example

Peter was a former marketing executive with Apple Computer, a credential which made him think he was smarter and more creative than everyone else in the startup company I had just joined. His high opinion of himself was exacerbated by the fact the company raised $20M in venture capital, partly because it had recruited Peter. He was the proverbial sacred cow. He could do no wrong. Few people dared to challenge his authority or directives.

I reported to a VP who reported to Peter. I was hired to manage electronic commerce. I was also responsible for building the company's website in preparation for the debut of the company's new software product. Peter never failed to remind me of where I fell in the food chain whenever I bumped into him in the halls. He would say, "Make sure you have me approve the content before publishing the website, okay?" or "Will I have to speak to your boss to make sure you make the launch date?"

Two weeks before launch, my team and I previewed the website to Peter as directed. He threw up all over it, specifically the download messaging and user interface for the free, trial version. There was no high-speed bandwidth in those days, so the size of the file was a key concern. We had designed the download to be able to happen in less than one minute at the most typical transfer speeds for the modems of the day. Peter overruled the design. He demanded we add high resolution graphics and additional functionality to the

trial version which quadrupled the size and, consequently, the time it took users to download.

Within days after the launch it was painfully apparent to all the company was
nowhere near the milestones it had set for itself for downloads and conver-
sions. My team was taking most of the heat for the lackluster response from
users. The board of directors called for a "post mortem" on the launch to determine why we were not hitting our targets. The day before I was scheduled
to present my report to the board, Peter came into my office and closed the
door. He asked me what I intended to say. He wanted to see my presentation.
I told him I was still working on it and had nothing to show him. He was miffed
and said, "Just keep it on the up-and-up because you know I can have you fired
if I wanted to."

The next day I entered the lion's den to face the board and give my account of
the ecommerce launch of the product via our website. It was generally believed
by most of the employees that heads would roll. I was the odd's-on favorite to
go first. I started my report but before I could finish, I was fielding a barrage of
questions from all sides of the room. Peter was particularly accusatory of how
the website was a "disaster" and the user abandon rates were the highest he
had ever seen in his career.

I calmly and deliberately answered every question. I owned up to the fact my
team had forecast 1,000 downloads per day, but the site was doing less than
100 downloads per day. I accepted responsibility for the poor performance.
Several board members shook their heads. Peter gloated in the back of the
room. He and I both figured the ax was ready to fall.

The company CEO asked me why I thought we were so far off our forecast. I
explained the size of the download was four times larger than originally
planned and the average user had to wait more than four minutes for the
download, rather than the industry accepted standard of one minute. He asked

me why the file size was so much bigger than originally intended. Without mentioning any names, I replied my team was directed to increase the size to accommodate high resolution graphics and more functionality.

With that comment, Peter spoke up to lay the blame at the feet of our webmaster. "That's why we pay Byron," Peter blurted out. "He is supposed to know better. He should have had your back and he should have advised the build team to keep the file size small." Peter winked at me, as if he was throwing me a life line. This was our bonding moment.

I paused deliberately, pulled two sheets of paper from my folder, held them up and said, "Well, Peter, I think you owe Byron an apology. This is a copy of his report advising us of exactly that. And this is a copy of your signature on the change order, overriding his recommendation and directing my team to increase the size of the download." I handed the papers to the CEO, who glanced at them quickly and passed them around to the other directors. Rather than admit he was wrong and apologizing to Byron, Peter doubled down on his position. "He obviously did not make the ramifications clear, otherwise I never would have authorized an increase in the download file size."

There would be no firing that day, but I knew I was now in Peter's crosshairs. It was only a matter of time before he mustered enough support to oust me. A few days later I was sitting in my office when Byron came in. He had heard I had stuck up for him at the board meeting and wanted to thank me. He said, "I thought you might want to visit this website when you get a chance." He slid a piece of paper to me with a URL printed on it, smiled, and walked out.

I called up the web site on my computer. It was a software consulting site owned by Peter and his partner, who also happened to be our chief legal counsel. He had been no prize to work with either. Apparently, the two of them were working part time on the side in violation of their employment contracts with our company. To make matters worse, one of the clients they listed on their web site was a fierce competitor of our company, a clear violation of their non-compete and non-disclosure agreements.

Byron was handing me two birds with one stone. They had been working their own gig very discreetly. They didn't figure anyone would find out. They didn't count on someone as Internet astute as Byron, who had a reason to set things right. I was more than obliged to bring it to the attention of the CEO. Peter and the company's chief legal counsel were let go the next day.

Moral of the story: people will find a way to get even with the people who are not self-aware enough to admit when they are wrong and, worse, try to blame it on others. A true professional would never give others a reason for sabotaging him, because he owns up to his mistakes and apologizes for them.

In the words of leadership guru, John C. Maxwell, "A man must be big enough to admit his mistakes, smart enough to profit from them, and strong enough to correct them."

Data point

Apology Steps

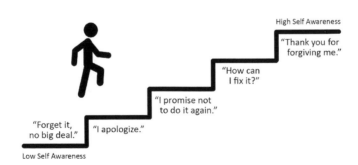

Source: The Ladder of Apology, Michael O'Donnell

It never ceases to amaze me how many people cannot admit when they are wrong, and they rarely apologize for anything, even the most egregious digressions. You probably know a few people like this yourself. They are shallow and insecure. Their egos prevent a healthy dose of humility. Some of them manage to ascend to positions of power and influence, but they are not respected or admired by those who know them best. It is not enough to apologize when wrong. True pros also vow to not to it again; fix it, and ask for forgiveness. They climb the ladder of apology to attain full redemption.

Strategies and tips for managing your temperament; admitting when you are wrong and apologizing.

 So how do you put this internalized behavior into practice?

First, train yourself not to react too quickly to people or situations at work. First instincts can be bad, especially if your instinct is to clobber someone physically or verbally. No matter what happens, what is said, or who says it, your first response should be to pause and take a deep breath, subtly. If the person or situation has angered you, excuse yourself if you can. Take a walk, calm down, and gather your thoughts and composure. A short pause or recess can do wonders to manage your temperament.

Second, use calming and quick assessment techniques. Some people count to ten. Some people use visualization to project themselves into a relaxed environment. Some people breathe in slowly and deeply to a count of eight, place their tongue on the inside bridge of their upper teeth, then exhale slowly to a count of eight. These techniques help you stay in control and allow you a moment to assess the person or situation. A quick assessment technique includes asking yourself, "What is the one thing I can do immediately to defuse this situation and/or get this person into a better frame of mind? Or, "This is another one for the books, what would x do?" where x is someone you respect and whom you have seen handle difficult situations and people.

Third, use humor and see an unsettling situation or person for what they probably are: funny or absurd. Learn to smile inwardly and say to yourself, "Wow, did she really just say that?" or "If this wasn't so funny or ridiculous, I might be tempted to lose my temper and put him in his place." Some professionals can crack a joke or make light of the situation to themselves or to the room, to keep things on an even keel. A related strategy is to welcome a tense situation with a sigh of resignation. You can say, "I'd like to get something off my chest and air it out before I do or say something I'll regret."

Fourth, never excuse yourself or others for bad temperament, or for failing to admit when you are wrong. When you say, "I've always had a short temper, I don't mean half of what I say, so get over it" you're basically communicating you have no self-control. Just because you admit to being ill-tempered, or too much pride to admit when you are wrong, does not make it okay for you to continue such behavior. Never excuse it in your partners, coworkers, or colleagues either. The first sign of one who is not self-aware is to always explain away or blame someone else for their bad temperament.

Fifth, learn how to argue effectively. Frustrations and habits of bad temperament develop because people do not know how to vent or express themselves in a positive manner. Knowing how to bring clarity to the issue and advocating for your point of view is a critical step towards managing your temperament. When you realize it's not about "winning" but about reasonable compromise and resolution, you will gain the edge over your temperament and the temperaments of those whom you are dealing with.

Sixth, never view being wrong as weakness, but as a humble show of your strength of character. Few things are more endearing to another than a professional who is "man enough" or "woman enough" to admit when he or she is wrong. Each time you admit you are wrong is one more reason you will likely be right when the same issue arises in a different context or setting. This one character flaw, the inability to admit when one is wrong, is what separates professionals from true professionals. When you are no longer afraid to admit when you are wrong, is the day you can look yourself in the mirror and say, "I'm not like most other professionals. I am a true professional."

Seventh, the only apology that is not a good one, is the one that is insincere or qualified with an excuse. When you apologize, be sincere and authentic. Express regret for the words or actions that caused it. Most importantly, say how you have learned from it and will do it differently the next time you are in the same situation. It's the people who say they are sorry over-and-over again, yet keep repeating the same bad behaviors, that never achieve the status of a true professional.

Finally, it is sometimes a wise strategy to apologize even when you are not wrong. I've seen true pros use this strategy brilliantly, to appease a valued employee, save an important account, or win over a new client. Sometimes there is a gray line between wrong and right. Extending your hand to someone while apologizing for whatever ill they felt slighted by, can be the defining moment that solidifies a profitable, long-term relationship.

The Final Word, by Lao Tzu[17]

"A great nation is like a great man: When he makes a mistake, he realizes it. Having realized it, he admits it. Having admitted it, he corrects it. He considers those who point out his faults as his most benevolent teachers. He thinks of his enemy as the shadow that he himself casts."

Good reads and resources

The Four Temperaments
by Rudolf Steiner and Peter Bridgmont

Please Understand Me II: Temperament, Character, Intelligence
by David Keirsey

Becoming Who We Are: Temperament and Personality in Development
by Mary K. Rothbart

The Five Languages of Apology: How to Experience Healing in all Your Relationships and When Sorry Isn't Enough
by Gary Chapman and Jennifer M. Thomas

Being Wrong: Adventures in the Margin of Error
by Kathryn Schulz

18. Know your weaknesses and blind spots; do not bluff.

One of the pioneers of the cell phone industry, Craig McCaw, said, *"I think the way I look at things gives me a different perspective. I'm most valuable when I work with a team of bright people who complement my weaknesses with their strengths."*

Accomplished people are keenly aware of their weaknesses and blind spots. Some work to overcome them. Others surround themselves with people who compensate for them. Whatever their strategies, successful people avoid the trap of denying their weaknesses or believing them to be unimportant. They do not try to hide them or bluff their way through something they do not know or cannot do. The true professional develops effective strategies for keeping their weaknesses from overshadowing their strengths.

What does it mean to know your weaknesses and blind spots, and to not bluff?

As a true professional, you know what you don't know. You know what you are naturally good at and what you are not naturally good at. You have taken various IQ, skills and personality assessments to illuminate your strengths and weaknesses and put them into perspective. You make a conscious effort to recruit and/or associate with people who can help you balance your strengths and weaknesses.

Whenever you are confronted with a question you cannot answer, or a problem you are presently ill-equipped to address, you don't try to fake it, especially if the stakes are high. You either defer to someone you know who has the answer or solution, or you defer it until you can address it with the right resources. You turn your weaknesses into strengths by first acknowledging them, second embracing them, and third counter-balancing them with the appropriate resources at your disposal.

A true example

One of Durward Owen's favorite sayings was, "Don't be oblivious to the obvious!" I contemplated this admonition when trying to decide whether I should shut down a venture I had just sunk two years of my life into and $100,000 in cash. One of the behaviors that is drilled into the head of every entrepreneur is "persistence". The mantra is, "Never give up...pivot...find a new way... make it work...just NEVER, EVER QUIT!" These are good and noble sentiments, but an experienced entrepreneur also knows that hope and passion alone are not enough to build a successful business. Neither is hard work in the absence of the right team and a competitive advantage.

My venture was called "Leaves" as in leaves on a family tree. The branches are what connect a person to his or her relatives, but most family trees are bare. They make the connections, but they don't tell the stories. The stories are the leaves on a family tree. I created a website and mobile app that made it easy for retirees to write their memoirs and to share their life stories with future generations. My software gave the older generation, who were not accustomed to using computers, a virtual biographer who interviewed them about their lives and the events that defined them. It also preserved digitally all of their memorabilia, like photo albums, family videos, birth and marriage certificates, and other important papers.

Soon after the beta launch, Facebook introduced a "Timeline" feature that enabled users to go back to any day and year, to record an entry. For the first time, a user's Facebook page was not just limited to recording the present moment, it could be used to document the user's past. At the same time, I was going through my third change of application designers and developers. I just couldn't seem to find the right mix of talent and chemistry that was required by the venture.

Because of my past entrepreneurial successes, I could have persuaded investors to fund the company, but I knew in my heart-of-hearts, that I would have to down play the company's weaknesses and bluff about its potential, now that it had lost the first-mover advantage. I shut the venture down. It wasn't, however, a total loss.

My parents had lost everything in Hurricane Katrina – 79 years of photo albums, family movies and other memories had been washed out to sea. While developing Leaves, I had recorded their life stories and recovered about half of their old photos by reaching out to their friends and other family members, who graciously made copies from their collections. My venture died a quick death, but my heritage will now live forever. I like to think of this story as an example of turning weaknesses into strengths. As Nelson Mandela once said, "I never lose. I either win or I learn."

Data point

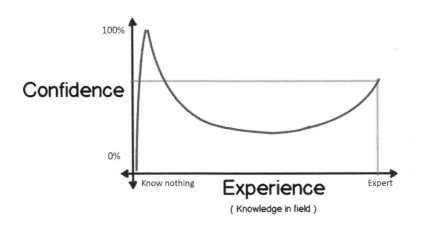

Source: The Dunning–Kruger Effect

The Dunning–Kruger effect is a cognitive bias in which low-ability individuals suffer from illusory superiority, mistakenly assessing their ability as much higher than it really is. Very simply, inept people fail to evaluate their strengths and competencies accurately. Ironically, Dunning-Kruger's research also suggests that high-ability individuals may underestimate their relative competence and may erroneously assume that tasks which are easy for them are also easy for others. The best way to avoid the Dunning-Kruger Effect is to conduct and independent assessment of your strengths and weaknesses every few years (see strategy #3).

Strategies and tips for knowing your weaknesses and blind spots, and not bluffing.

 So how do you put this internalized behavior into practice?

First, actively seek out and associate with people who are not like yourself. Blind spots occur when you hire people or hang out with people like yourself. It is how group think and myopia develop. A true professional will hire and associate with his or her opposites. Only 15 percent of your success will be determined by job knowledge and technical skills. 85 percent will be determined by your attitude, relationships, and ability to relate to other people.

Second, realize that your strengths may create corresponding weaknesses and blind spots. Your natural gifts are also liabilities. For example, if you are very spontaneous and decisive, that can be both good and bad, depending upon the situation. Strengths can be weaknesses in disguise, and vice versa. If you are analytical, deliberate and cautious, that strength could also be a disadvantage in a situation that calls for immediate action in the absence of all the information necessary to make the ideal decision.

Third, take scientifically-validated assessments every 3-5 years. You are not the same person you were 3-5 years ago. You will not be the same person 3-5 years from now that you are today. A true professional is always growing in knowledge, psychology, and self-awareness. The present is not the past. Times have changed, you have changed. Check-in with yourself from time-to-time to see how your strengths and weaknesses have evolved. Pay special attention to your "derailers," the weaknesses and blind spots that could negatively impact your professional career.

Fourth, have at least one solid relationship with a trusted colleague who knows you professionally and whom you see as your equal. This person is your "reality check". You need to be brutally honest with this person, and he or she with you. If you are fortunate enough to have a mentor, this is the most important role he or she can play in your career. A good mentor will tell you what you might not want to hear, and you will not be upset or defensive in hearing it from him or her.

Fifth, build or adopt tools which help compensate for your weaknesses and blind spots. After listing your weaknesses and blind spots, or receiving an independent assessment of them, implement the tools that counter them and use them daily. For example, if one of your weaknesses is always running late, use the calendar and alarm on your phone for EVERY appointment. If one of your weaknesses is procrastination, sign up for an email or text service that will prompt you on your goals and milestones EVERY day.

Sixth, memorize and repeat certain triggers to yourself, or state them aloud to your colleagues when the situation calls for them. For example, if one of your weaknesses is the inability to say "no" when your boss or coworkers asks you to do something, get into the habit of replying, "I think I can accommodate that, but before I say yes, let me check my to-do list and other commitments." If one of your blind spots is cynicism or mistrust, whenever a colleague says something you are immediately skeptical of, say, "I'll take you at your word unless the facts prove otherwise."

Seventh, if you do bluff and someone calls it, don't double down on it. Swallow your pride and say something like, "Yes, I knew better when I said it, but my pride got the best of me." or "I should have given that some more thought before saying it, my apologies." Trouble always ensues and can severely damage a professional reputation, when one tries to deny, obfuscate or cover up a bluff when it is called. The satirist, Ambrose Bierce, perhaps said it best, "The hardest tumble a man can take is to fall over his own bluff." Sticking with a bluff after it's been called, or stating a mistruth over-and-over in the belief that if you say it enough, people will believe it, is a recipe for professional suicide. Heed the lessons from Behavior #17, admit when you are wrong and apologize.

Finally, be aware of confirmation bias and hindsight bias. They are common blind spots. Be aware of the human tendency to process information in a way that fits one's world view. As the acclaimed investor, Warren Buffett says, "What the human being is best at doing, is interpreting all new information so that their prior conclusions remain intact." Be aware of the human tendency to supplement fresh thinking with hindsight thinking. Whenever you hear yourself saying, "That's the way we have always done it." or "It's always worked for me in the past", a little warning bell should go off in your mind.

The Final Word, by James A. Owen[18]

"Admitting your faults isn't a weakness – it's a strength. Having your weaknesses pointed out isn't a slur on your character – it's an opportunity to improve your life."

Good reads and resources

Leadership Blindspots: How Successful Leaders Identify and Overcome the Weaknesses That Matter
by Robert Bruce Shaw

Blindspot: Hidden Biases of Good People
by Mahzarin R. Banaji and Anthony G. Greenwald

Blind Spots: Why We Fail to Do What's Right and What to Do about It
by Max H. Bazerman and Ann E. Tenbrunsel

Weakness To Winning: Tools to Kill Negative Thoughts and Habits Preventing You from Living Your Purpose
by J.C. Nix and Tammy Kling

Truth vs Falsehood: How to Tell the Difference
by David R. Hawkins

19. Be mindful of yourself in different environments; adapt, but do not make uninformed assumptions.

"It ain't what you don't know that gets you into trouble. It's what you know for sure that just ain't so." – Mark Twain

Successful people have the presence of mind to adapt their thinking and approaches depending upon the environment and who is present. They can be outgoing and forward or subdued and reflective, depending upon whom they are with and what the situation calls for. They can change the way they view the world based upon new experiences. No matter how important they are in their world, they don't assume everyone they meet knows who they are or even cares.

True professionals are acutely aware of themselves in different situations and how to adapt themselves accordingly. They don't insist the environment adapt to them, they adapt to their environment. Their success is based partly on their flexibility and versatility. They train themselves not to make quick, uninformed assumptions about others. They are not one-size-fits-all professionals. Their mindful demeanor and flexible approach enables them to move like chameleons through any professional gathering.

What does it mean to be mindful of yourself in different environments; adapting, but not making uninformed assumptions?

As a true professional, you don't think you have everyone figured out, especially when meeting them for the first time. You don't automatically go into "sales mode" or "know-it-all" mode. You can take the lead or defer to others, depending upon what the situation calls for. You don't have a pat role you always play. You can break character and adapt yourself to different environments.

In meetings with new associates, you don't assume the protocols are the same as they are for meetings in your own organization. When traveling abroad you don't assume people there have the same attitudes and outlooks as people in your country. When confronted with a problem you don't immediately assume the worse. When someone challenges you, you don't immediately assume they are out to get you. You practice the art of patience and restraint, so that you can adapt and make the appropriate, measured response. Your peers and colleagues often comment how flexible and adaptive you are in different situations.

A true example

In the span of one day, I watched Eric navigate multiple meetings with different people in different environments as if he were three different people. It was truly a marvel to witness. I served with Eric on the board of directors of the Northwest Entrepreneurs Network. Eric was a successful business attorney. Most of his clients were young entrepreneurs who were running fast growth technology companies. He had a thriving practice serving a very high maintenance and demanding clientele. We were the co-chairs of the organization's signature annual event: Entrepreneur University. It was a sellout crowd.

In the morning, Eric kicked off the event as one of the Master of Ceremonies. He laid out the day's schedule, introduced the special guests in attendance, and thanked the staff for their hard work organizing the event. He infused self-effacing "lawyer humor" with an authoritative review of the goals and expectations for the day. He was every bit in command of the stage, but his presence illuminated others. He was the thoughtful host.

In the afternoon, in one of the breakout rooms, Eric moderated a panel of startup founders about attracting and compensating talent. The panelists, all newly-minted CEO's, engaged in a vigorous debate. Each tried to one-up the other by touting their respective recruitment success stories. Eric was masterful in controlling the debate and countering showmanship. He knew his role was not to highlight or appease the panelists, who were his clients, or to inter- ject his own knowledge on the subject, which was substantial. His role was to deliver value to the audience. He was brilliant at surfacing different perspec- tives and takeaways. He was the effective facilitator.

In the evening at the closing reception, I watched Eric work the room like a seasoned politician. In each corner of the room, over several hours, he greeted people warmly and made introductions to those who did not know each other. As I entered one of the circles he immediately introduced me to those I did not know and began touting my praises, before turning his attention to tout the praises of another. He was the courteous colleague and connector.

It occurred to me later how much more aware and mindful Eric was than others I have watched in similar environments. In those situations, the "leaders" al- ways felt a need to lead. They were always "on stage". They insisted on holding court, dominating the conversation, and making it about "them". With Eric, it was always about those whom he was working with, never about himself. That awareness, in fact, spoke more about him than he could ever say about him- self. He was a true pro, liked and respected by his clients and colleagues alike.

Data Point

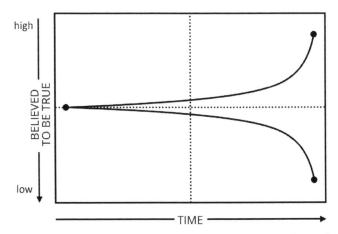

Source: Rick Smith, The Only Innovation Metric that Matters: Speed to Truth

Many people make snap judgements based on uniformed assumptions. Rather than starting on the neutral line, as depicted in the graph above, they start high or low and immediately believe something to be true or untrue. Over time, they find out if they were right or wrong. True professionals train themselves not to make snap judgements. They don't assume. They allow adequate time for accurate information and assessment before making a judgment.

Strategies and tips for being mindful in different environments; adapting, but not making uninformed assumptions.

 So how do you put this internalized behavior into practice?

First, be aware of stereotypes and train yourself not to fall victim to them. Whether it is gender, age, title or status, ethnicity or culture, remind yourself that every environment and every person is unique. Do not expect people to talk or behave in a certain way. Approach all people and situations, especially in professional environments, as a clean slate. Conversely, if someone tries to paint you with a stereotype be quick to disavow them of the notion. For example, when some people find out I am of Irish heritage, they often remark how much I must like pubs. I usually reply, "I suppose I like pubs as much as the next guy, but not as much as a good glass of red wine."

Second, ask questions first, offer thoughts and opinions second. Learn about your environment. Assess the people and the situation. You wouldn't walk into the public library with a boom box on your shoulder blasting rap music. People who blunder into situations and embarrass themselves (or their companies) are simply not mindful of their surroundings. They are too self-absorbed to read the situation. They are literally out of tune. Don't be one of those people!

Third, before meeting a new colleague or client, do a little research. Find out something interesting about them and ask them about it at the appropriate moment. For example, when meeting someone for the first time I often remark about their favorite subject or sports team. It was easy to find on social media. Bridge that awkward new acquaintance gap by finding something you have in common. Of course, just because you find out they attended a certain school don't assume they even follow their alma mater's sports teams. Verify first. If you can't find proof of their interests ahead of time simply ask, "Are you following the team this season?"

Fourth, the most important aspect of being mindful is silence. If you are with others, it allows you to listen and concentrate. It prompts you to clarify before assuming. If you are in a new environment, sitting or standing by yourself while others mill around, silence allows you to breath in the energy. It allows you to observe the sights and sounds. It gives you a chance to read faces and body language. When you are silent and observant, you are truly present.

Fifth, adapting successfully to a new environment or stressful situation requires three things: openness, flexibility, and suspending judgment. These are the mental supports of a mindful professional. True professionals don't believe they should have everyone and everything figured out; they can go with the flow. They don't judge, they experience. Even in difficult situations a true professional believes in the probability of a positive outcome.

Sixth, avoid the tendency to see things as black or white. Life is a thousand shades of grey and more than 10 million colors, all at the same time. People are not robots; no two think or act alike. People and environments are also constantly changing. A second encounter with them can be a much different experience. If you "assume" they will be one way, you will be thrown off balance when they don't meet your expectations. The professionals who begin to lose their edge are usually those who start to quickly classify and categorize people and events into nice, neat little compartments.

Seventh, this is an easy one, but also easy to forget: people are NOT like you. They don't like the same things as you do. They don't have the same goals, priorities or aspirations. They may not have the same morals or values as you do. This does not make them right or wrong, better or worse. It makes them different than you; period. It makes them....them. Too many people tune out those who think differently, believe differently, behave differently, and live differently. It is an affront to their own identity and sense of self. True professionals overcome these insecurities. They embrace diversity and celebrate their differences with others.

Finally, a word of caution. If you get very good at adapting to different environments and empathizing with all people, you may start to become a different person. Hopefully, you will become a more thoughtful and aware person.

The danger is losing yourself altogether. Adapting to others does not mean becoming them. It means understanding them and relating to them. It's important to stay centered. Be ever aware of your own special place in the world.

The Final Word, by Dolly Parton[19]

"We cannot direct the wind, but we can adjust the sails."

Good reads and resources

The Four Agreements: A Practical Guide to Personal Freedom
by Miguel Ruiz

Who Moved My Cheese?: An Amazing Way to Deal with Change in Your Work and in Your Life
by Spencer Johnson and Kenneth Blanchard

The Power of Awareness
by Neville Goddard

Managing Oneself (Harvard Business Review Classics)
by Peter Ferdinand Drucker

The Healthy Habit Revolution: Create Better Habits in 5 Minutes a Day
by Derek Doepker

20. Get out of your comfort zone; change it up, seek new and challenging experiences.

> The actor, motivational speaker and former U.S. Army soldier, J. R. Martinez, said, *"I've learned in my life that it's important to be able to step outside your comfort zone and be challenged with something you're not familiar or accustomed to. That challenge will allow you to see what you can do."*

One of the marks of true professionals is they have so few regrets. As soon as they feel they are becoming stale or complacent they change things up. They are not afraid of taking calculated risks. They seek out new and challenging experiences. They believe one is either busy being born or busy dying. They are aware of their own inertia: physically, intellectually, emotionally, and spiritually. They would rather try something and be wrong than do nothing and always be right.

This is not to say professionals take foolish risks and spontaneously fly off in a new direction on a whim. Most of them stick to what they know and love, but keep getting better at it. They find new outlets to express their creativity. They stay curious. They take to heart the advice of Supreme Court Justice, Oliver Wendell Holmes, Jr.: "A mind that is stretched by a new experience can never go back to its old dimensions."

What does it mean to get out of your comfort zone, change it up, and seek new and challenging experiences?

As a true professional, you don't rest on your laurels. As soon as you achieve a goal or milestone, you set a new one. You take on new assignments at work, especially those that stretch you. When you feel yourself getting bored and slipping into a dull routine you look for ways to change things up. You reorganize your office or transfer to a new office. You accept a new position, even if it's not as glamorous as the one you have.

Over time you find the right balance between growth and comfort. You push yourself, but not too fast or too hard. You're not afraid to ease into a new experience or use a safety net. You enjoy your comforts and conveniences but you don't allow them to age you or control you. There is almost nothing you can't live without. You value new people, places and experiences over acquiring and hoarding things.

A true example

After selling my second company I had two challenging, back-to-back jobs in other high tech companies. While at the second job I had the opportunity to incubate a concept for a new product. The CEO was wise enough to give me time to work on it in between my regular duties. He was ahead of his time. This was before it became common practice in many companies to allow employees to spend up to 20% of their time doing whatever they wanted to work on.

The market research and product prototype I produced proved to be very promising. It was off plan for what the CEO wanted to do for his company, so he suggested I spin it out as its own business. We agreed the company I worked for would take 15% ownership in the new entity for having incubated it. At the same time I was offered an executive position in a hot new venture which had just raised $40M in venture capital.

At this point I was faced with a difficult choice. I could stay with the company I was with which was on a good path, leave to work on the new business being spun out, or I could take the new higher paying job with the hot, well-funded startup. I had gotten used to a very good, steady paycheck. I had also gotten used to a good health plan and other benefits. I harkened back to my first two companies when I did not have those things and wondered if I could go back to that uncertainty. I was also raising three kids who required an ever-increasing amount of time and money.

The night before I was to give an answer to the hot, well-funded startup, my wife and I sat up all night and talked about the options. We laid on the couch facing each other, our feet touching. We literally sat there and talked from the time the kids went to bed at 10:00 pm until 6:00 am the next morning. We talked about how far we had come, what a nice life we were providing for our children, and what we wanted for our collective futures. By 6:00 am we had decided: I was going to take the high paying job with the hot, well-funded startup. It meant a lot more money, full benefits, more responsibility, and a fair amount of professional prestige. It was the most lucrative, safest bet.

At 8:30 am I walked into the offices of the founder and CEO of the hot, well-funded company for our scheduled appointment. He was beaming and seemed delighted to see me. He was anxious to welcome me aboard and get me up to speed. He started telling me all the plans he had to build his dream company. At that moment, it became crystal clear to me. The CEO sensed my thoughts. He stopped midsentence and said, "What?"

I looked at him thoughtfully and replied, "I am very sorry, and I know I might regret it later, but I am going to pass on your generous offer. I am going to start my own company." He smiled the way like-minded entrepreneurs do with each other. He knew my mind and my heart. He wished me luck. I wished him luck. We shook hands and I left to call my wife to tell her what I had done. Bless her heart. She said, "If that's what you really want to do, then go do it."

One week later I was working as the sole employee of the spin out company. No paycheck, no benefits, but as invigorated as I had been in a long time. This story isn't just about getting out of your comfort zone. It's also about trusting your instincts and staying true to YOUR dreams so you don't end up devoting your life to someone else's dreams.

Data point

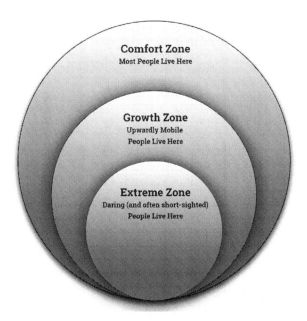

Chances are, just about everyone you know can be grouped into one of the three zones depicted in this chart. The clear majority of people, at least 70%, live in the Comfort Zone. Most of us like it there because…well, it's comfortable. A small subset of people, less than 10%, live in the Extreme Zone. They are adrenaline junkies. They are not happy unless they are putting it all on the line all the time. The sweet spot is the Growth Zone. Only about 20% of the people live there. Most of them are the ones that rise to the top of their professions. Strive to be a twenty-percenter.

Strategies and tips for getting out of your comfort zone, changing it up, and seeking new and challenging experiences.

 So how do you put this adaptive behavior into practice?

First, be aware of your mind's love of convenient rationalization. It's convenient to think something is too risky, unimportant, or not worth the effort. It's always easier and safer to do nothing. You can talk yourself out of most anything if you allow yourself to do so. The aware professional does not dismiss the new and unknown so quickly. It's something you must train your mind to do.

Second, ask yourself, "What's the worst that could happen?" If the answer is "death" or "professional suicide" well then, you will want to think about it very carefully. If the worst thing that could happen is losing a little time or money, but perhaps learning something new or gaining new colleagues, then it's usually counterproductive to over think it.

Third, have a goal, a plan, a budget and some deadlines. People who make abrupt changes or go into something blind are often disappointed. The idea is to go into it with reasonable expectations for the experience and a plan to achieve the desired outcomes. You can then reassess as you progress. You can't assess whether it was a good move or a bad move if you didn't first frame what success looks like.

Fourth, define the parameters of your comfort zone. You don't have to move it by miles; move it by feet, expand it gradually. If you are terrified by the prospect of going into debt, determine in advance the amount of money you are willing to risk. Your comfort zone can always have a safety net in the event you do fall. If you know you can recover from the fall it won't scare you out of making the leap.

Fifth, change it up by doing something out of the ordinary. It doesn't have to be something professional. Just do something completely different, something you have never done before. Take scuba diving lessons, or dance lessons. Paint. Learn to play an instrument. The act of doing something completely new and different, either professionally or personally, will stimulate your creative juices and help you see the world in a fresh new light.

Sixth, enroll others in your new adventure. Whether you decide to travel to a foreign place, build something, or transition to a new career, ask others to "follow" you and give you feedback. Some people do this by blogging about it. Others share their new experience via social media. They invite others to virtually go on the new journey with them. It will inspire them while supporting you.

Seventh, take the leap with no expectations whatsoever. This is the counterstrategy to number three above. You wouldn't want to risk everything with this strategy, but you can do something benign just for the heck of it, then see what happens. Say to yourself, "I have zero expectations for this experience. I'm simply going to do it for my senses. I'm going to see it, hear it, smell it, taste it and feel it, with NO preconceived notions at all." You might just surprise yourself.

Finally, keep a diary of your private thoughts and feelings. Whenever you are trying something completely new, something out of your comfort zone, it is therapeutic to document it and have conversations with yourself. This will help you to become more self-aware. It will help you to surface your fears and to stare them down. Be your own best friend. Get better acquainted with yourself. Go back and read what you wrote to yourself several years earlier. You will probably laugh. You might cry. But most importantly, you will gain new insights into yourself.

The Final Word, by Vanessa Hudgens[20]

> "I just love expanding my horizons and growing as an artist. The only way you get to do that is by doing something that scares you or takes you out of your comfort zone."

Good reads and resources

Trajectory: 7 Career Strategies To Take You From Where You Are To Where You Want To Be
by David Van Rooy

The Untethered Soul: The Journey Beyond Yourself
by Michael A. Singer

Your comfort zone is killing you: Finding the courage to be you
by Billy Anderson

Do One Thing Every Day That Scares You: A Journal
by Robie Rogge and Dian Smith

The Big Leap: Conquer Your Hidden Fear and Take Life to the Next Level
by Hendricks, Gay, PhD

Hillbilly Elegy: A Memoir of a Family and Culture in Crisis
by J. D. Vance

CHAPTER 5

TIMELY

This is the PROACTIVE you, how you get things done and stay <u>responsive</u> to change.

It's about time management, organization, preparation and perseverance, timeliness, responsiveness and closure.

21. Be on time and use time wisely; do not procrastinate.

The Pulitzer Prize writer, Carl Sandburg, wrote, *"Time is the most valuable coin in your life. You and you alone will determine how that coin will be spent. Be careful that you do not let other people spend it for you."*

Good time management is more than just an idiom to successful professionals; it is a way of life. It is a non-negotiable habit. It is internalized into their thinking and engrained into their behavioral patterns. They see time as one of their most precious resources and the thing that puts them on an even playing field with every other human being. Successful professionals don't waste time. They don't put things off. They have a reputation for meeting deadlines and getting things done on schedule.

What does it mean to be on time, to use time wisely, and to not procrastinate?

As a true professional, you are almost never late for any meeting or event. Your colleagues joke they can set their watches by you. When you are going to be late, which is unavoidable from time to time, you call or text the people you are scheduled to meet with to let them know you are running late. When you arrive late, you apologize profusely and make it clear that being on time is one of your pet peeves. You never give any of your colleagues or associates the impression it's okay to keep them waiting, or your time is more valuable than theirs.

Over the years you have trained yourself to do what must be done, when it needs to be done, whether you like doing it or not. In fact, you make a point of getting the unpleasant but necessary tasks out of the way before tackling the things you like to do. You are not necessarily a clock watcher, but you are acutely aware time is one of your most competitive advantages. Your colleagues and your associates appreciate you because you value and appreciate their time. You don't waste your time or theirs. Conversely, you avoid people who suck up your time and distract you from the important tasks at hand.

A True example

Bradford was always running behind. He was my director of marketing and sales. He usually walked into every staff meeting at least five minutes late. He never apologized, but always had a good excuse. "I was on the phone with a client" he would say, or "My last meeting ran behind". I never called him on it because he was a good natured guy, very competent and well liked by all. I didn't want to dampen his enthusiasm or come across as an overly demanding boss. His bad habit of being persistently late for staff meetings could be over-looked and forgiven, I thought. I had bigger things to worry about.

Several months later I made a surprise visit to our booth at an industry trade show. I hadn't been expected to attend, but my schedule changed and I figured I would take the opportunity to attend the conference and work the booth for a few days. I missed the days when I worked our trade booth for eight hours every day for three days straight. I loved meeting our customers and partners and demonstrating the product. I showed up on the first day and looked for our booth when the exhibit doors opened. It wasn't set up; nothing but drapery and carpet. I tracked down someone in exhibitor services and asked them why our booth wasn't set up. "We just got the work order this morning," he said. "I'll send someone over." I tried to reach Bradford on his cell. No answer.

About an hour later exhibitor services found our exhibit crates in the back and had set up the booth. I was demonstrating our product to a few conference attendees when Bradford strolled into the booth. He looked surprised to see me. After attending to the customers, I confronted him about why our booth was not set up on time and why he was late. He said he had gotten the set up time mixed up on his itinerary and blamed his assistant for not making arrange-ments with exhibitor services. I ended up working the booth for the next two days. Both days Bradford was at least five minutes late.

When I got back to the office I had a private meeting with his assistant. She conceded she had a miscue with Bradford on dates and times for the exhibit set up. That meeting led me to meet privately with other members of our marketing and sales team. They all reported similar behavior patterns. Bradford was typically five to ten minutes late for his own staff meetings. He was also consistently late with meetings with our vendors and customers. Everyone liked him and thought he did a good job, but conceded he had a bad habit of being late. It was systemic in his behavior.

I had a heart to heart talk with Bradford. I told him I could not keep him on. While not fatal to the business, his persistent tardiness was not good for staff morale. I also didn't want a reputation with customers and vendors that we seemed to value our time more highly than theirs. His behavior reflected on me and the company. To his credit, he admitted his tardiness had always been a problem. He vowed to do better. Against my better judgment, I said I would give him one more chance. I made it very clear to him this was not one of several warnings. If it happened one more time, he was gone. No reprieve, no promises to do better. Good intentions without real change would not be acceptable. He agreed.

This was one of those times I was glad that my better judgment had been wrong. Bradford was never late for another meeting: with me, his staff, or our customers or vendors (I checked). In fact, he was often five minutes early. About a year later I asked him how he did it. He told me he underwent hypnosis therapy and made it a priority in his life. He thanked me and said it was the best change he had ever made in himself.

Data point

Leisure time on an average day

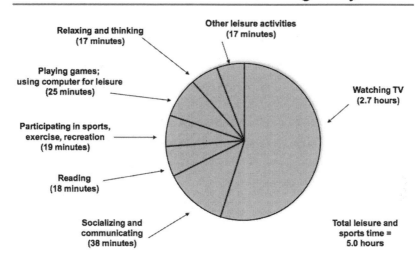

Relaxing and thinking
(17 minutes)

Other leisure activities
(17 minutes)

Playing games;
using computer for leisure
(25 minutes)

Watching TV
(2.7 hours)

Participating in sports,
exercise, recreation
(19 minutes)

Reading
(18 minutes)

Socializing and
communicating
(38 minutes)

Total leisure and
sports time =
5.0 hours

Source: Bureau of Labor Statistics latest American Time Use Survey

Most people spend more than half of their spare time watching television. It equates to about nine years of one's natural life. Many people complain there is not enough time to do what they want to do – learn a new skill, start a business, or take classes. The data suggests there is plenty of time; most people simply choose to use it poorly. What could you do with those nine years?

Strategies and tips for being on time, using time wisely, and overcoming the tendency to procrastinate.

 So how do you put this internalized behavior into practice?

First, realize persistent tardiness and poor time management is a choice...a bad habit. It's not something you were born with, nor are you resigned to it. Likewise, a habit of putting things off that you know you should do is also a bad habit. If you excuse it and tolerate it in yourself, you will have to excuse it and tolerate it in your colleagues, employees and associates. And that could be your undoing. The first strategy is to stop excusing it and make time management a priority in your life.

Second, always budget for buffer time. If you know the commute is usually 20 minutes, give yourself 30 minutes. If the meeting is scheduled to start at 9:00 am, plan to arrive at 8:50 am. If necessary, set your watch to run 10 minutes ahead. Set your alarm to go off with an appropriate buffer time. Resist the tendency to think arriving early makes you look weak or eager. It is those who always arrive late who are weak of character and unprofessional.

Third, employ a virtual assistant. There are people who do this for a living for a low monthly fee. If you can't afford a real assistant, use a virtual assistant tool. These tools sync with your calendar. They will send you text notifications and even call you to remind you of meetings and tasks. Make sure all your devices – laptop, phone, tablet, watch – are synchronized with the same calendar and set for the same time.

Fourth, to use time wisely, learn to delegate. There are a whole lot of things you can get others to do for you. You can either pay them or exchange favors. Use your mate, parents, kids, neighbors, friends and associates. All successful people figure out how to delegate daily tasks and offload the less important or routine duties to others.

Fifth, to use time wisely you should have written short term and long term goals and objectives. Keep these on your phone or on a piece of paper in your wallet. Read them daily. Know what needs to be done each day to bring you one step closer to your goals. Prioritize daily. Being busy for the sake of being busy is counterproductive if you are not busy doing the right things. This also means budgeting down time when you need it.

Sixth, to overcome procrastination, develop your own system of rewards and punishments. If you reward yourself whether you accomplish something or not, you are simply reinforcing a bad habit. You must postpone gratification until the things that need to be done get done. Enroll your friends and associates in helping you achieve your goals and completing your tasks. Invite them to celebrate with you when they are achieved.

Seventh, break tasks into manageable parts so you don't get overwhelmed with what must be done. Reward yourself on incremental achievements. A big project at work does not get done in one day. It usually gets done by breaking it down into pieces and assigning different people to different pieces. The same strategy can be used for managing your own projects. This book, for example, was not written in a few days. It took months by focusing on writing just one or two pages each day.

Finally, almost nothing important gets done without a deadline. More specifically, nothing gets done without a series of small deadlines. Set a reasonable deadline for completion of the total project. Work your way backwards to identify all the incremental deadlines you must meet to meet the big deadline. When you miss an incremental deadline, don't panic. Assess your progress and adjust the deadlines accordingly. Stay in control of time. It is something you should always manage. Never let it manage you.

The Final Word, by Anthony Robbins[21]

"Once you have mastered time, you will understand how true it is that most people overestimate what they can accomplish in a year – and underestimate what they can achieve in a decade!"

Good reads and resources

Get It Done: 39 Actionable Tips to Increase Productivity Instantly and Stop Procrastination!
by Steve Xavier

Eat That Frog!: 21 Great Ways to Stop Procrastinating and Get More Done in Less Time
by Brian Tracy

Procrastination: Why You Do It, What to Do About It Now
by Jane B. Burka and Lenora M. Yuen

The Motivation Switch: 77 Ways to Get Motivated, Avoid Procrastination, and Achieve Success
by AJ Winters

22. Be organized; make a "To Do" list every day and separate the important from the unimportant.

The French poet and novelist, Victor Hugo, wrote, *"He who every morning plans the transactions of that day and follows that plan carries a thread that will guide him through the labyrinth of the most busy life."*

The most important time management technique used by busy, successful professionals, is using a to-do list every day. This one behavior stands alone as the key to success for many people. They don't even have to think about doing it each day; it's automatic. They make a list at the same time every day, as habitual as eating, drinking and sleeping. They get very good at filtering the list to determine the important from the unimportant, then plan their time and efforts accordingly. True professionals are indeed busy, but they are usually busy doing the things that matter. As Henry David Thoreau wrote, "It's not enough to be busy, so are the ants. The question is: what are we busy about?"

What does it mean to be organized, make a "To Do" list every day and separate the important from the unimportant?

As a true professional you are very good at compartmentalizing your daily to-dos according to your personal life and professional life. You don't rely solely on your memory. It's not a mental list, it's a physical one. The act of writing them out makes them real, not an afterthought. You write down the things that need to get done, and then you prioritize their order and importance.

Your daily to-do list is in sync with your larger goals and objectives, especially those which provide your living. You test your list against how well it moves you closer to your important goals. If something on your list must get done but is relatively unimportant in the scheme of things, you try to delegate it. As you assess your list each day, you figure out how to accomplish it with the least amount of wasted time and effort. You see your time as your most valuable resource and you are determined not to squander it on unimportant matters.

A true example

After working two years for Durward Owen I had become accustomed to making a to-do list every evening before bed. I always had a few books and a pad and pen sitting on the nightstand next to my bed. My routine was to read each evening for an hour or so (one of the other behaviors of a true professional), and then write down my to-dos for the following day. I found doing it right before bed allowed my subconscious to work on them while I slept.

At first it was difficult to fall asleep because writing my list for the following day would get my mind to thinking about them. I would visualize doing them. I got excited (sometimes anxious) about all I had to do. I wanted to get started now. I experimented with writing my to-do list in the morning, but I always felt rushed and thought the list was not as thorough and on point as the ones I wrote before bed. I finally found a solution to this dilemma. The very first thing I wrote on my to-do list each evening was: "Get a good night's sleep!"

The next day over breakfast or on my daily commute I would read the list again. I got in the habit of placing an A, B, or C next to each item. The A's were the things that had to get done and were usually the first things I focused on, but not always. If something on the list was less important but needed to be done first, I tried to complete it quickly. I always made little notes next to each item; thoughts on who to talk to or how to complete the task. Over the years I transitioned from using a pen and pad to making the list and notes on my mobile phone each day, but I stayed committed to this behavior.

Later in my career I discovered another effective technique. For the most important things that needed to be done at work each day I wrote on a huge white board in my office. I wrote them so that EVERYONE in my company could see them. My colleagues would often comment on them. I was publicly holding myself accountable to my tasks and I was inviting my coworkers to help hold me accountable as well.

I can honestly testify this behavior, and these techniques, made me appear to some as superhuman. Year in and year out I effectively ran a growing company, served on the boards of several nonprofits, wrote books, articles and white papers which were published, stayed in good physical condition, and spent plenty of quality time with my family and friends.

Throughout my career the advice of Durward Owen often reverberated in my mind: "If you want to get something done, ask a busy person." I wanted to be the professional other people could count on to get things done. And, to a large extent, I succeeded because of my daily to-do list.

Data point

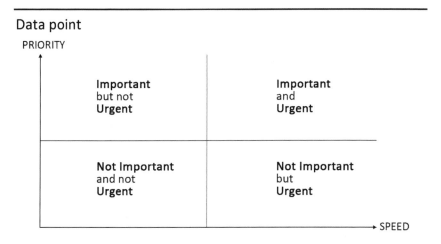

Source: First suggested by President Dwight B. Eisenhower. Later popularized in the book, "The Seven Habits of Highly Effective People."

True professionals organize their workload and priorities appropriately. President Dwight D. Eisenhower famously said, "I have two kinds of problems: the urgent and the important. The urgent are not important, and the important are never urgent." Important activities have an outcome that lead you to achieve your goals, especially your professional goals. Urgent activities demand immediate attention, and are usually associated with achieving someone else's goals – like your boss' goals. The consequences of not dealing with them are immediate.

The trick is to know which things fall into which quadrant. The lower-left quadrant are usually routine things, or sometimes they are just busy work. Try to cancel them, automate them or delegate them. The things in the upper left quadrant are usually your long-term goals and aspirations. They should remain your biggest priorities. It's easy to lose sight of them and not stay attentive to them. Keep them front and center and make steady progress on them

The things in the lower right hand quadrant are usually the things that prevent you from accomplishing your goals. They represent the drama and mini-crisis's others attempt to saddle you with. Try to dispense with them quickly, or deflect them. The upper right quadrant often demands your immediate time and you often must attend to them. Don't let them consume you. They should be few and occasional. If you are spending all your time on these things, you might want to reassess your job or relationships.

Strategies and tips for being organized; making a to-do list every day and separating the important from the unimportant.

 So how do you put this internalized behavior into practice?

First, make your list every day at the same time. Do it whenever it works best for you. As I wrote above, I like to make mine before bed. Other people like to make theirs before they leave work to go home each evening. Just get into the rhythm of doing it at roughly the same time each day.

Second, keep your to-do list as SHORT as possible. A long list is counterproductive. No need to write down all the menial things you need to do each day. A list of 3-6 items is manageable, and they should be the most important things to do for the day. Keep your list high impact.

Third, if you are new to making a to-list, start with the things you know you can accomplish. Condition yourself for success. If you have a long list of very hard things, you will likely fail. It becomes a vicious cycle, so you stop doing it. Create a virtuous circle by accomplishing and checking things off your list.

Fourth, recycle the uncompleted tasks. You are going to have bad days. You are going to get ill. You are going to have surprises and distractions that take you off task. No problem. If something important does not get done, put it right back on the list for the following day. Don't let them slide by convincing yourself they were not all that important to begin with. Train your mind. If something makes it on the list, you will get it done no matter what.

Fifth, schedule uninterrupted time each day. The reason many professionals fail to complete their to-do lists is because they allow others to hijack their time. Whether it is your boss, spouse, kids, or coworkers you need to set boundaries and make the time to complete the tasks you set for yourself before helping others complete their list. What is important to others should not automatically be important to you, so don't let anyone reset your priorities. Put them down the list to do if you have time after completing what's important to you.

Sixth, every so often, do a brain dump. Your daily list should be reasonably short, but it can be organized and prioritized against a very long list of things rattling around in your brain. Get them all out, don't let them fester in the recesses of your mind. Make a list of 100 things if you must. Look at it objectively. Compartmentalize the list into professional, personal, family, social, etc. Cross some things off, prioritize the other things. This exercise will help bring clarity to your daily to-do list.

Seventh, simplify and automate the routine. There are a bunch of routine things that need to get done each day: brush your teeth, get dressed, find your keys, charge your cell phone, stop at the store, pay your bills, etc. These things can distract from your important to-do list. What blows my mind is how many people reinvent doing these things every day and spend inordinate amounts of wasted time to do them. The smart professional simplifies and automates these routine tasks. They shave in the shower, hang their keys in the same place every day, plug in their devices right before going to bed using the same outlet, lay out their clothes for the next day, set up their bills to be paid automatically each month, etc.

Finally, every so often, conduct a time management audit. Keep your to-do lists and page through them once or twice a year. Assess what you spent your time on each week. Measure those things with how much they helped you achieve your long-term goals for professional development and career advancement.

The Final Word, by Heidi Klum[22]

"I'm a big believer in to-do lists. I think of five things in the shower. I set goals and get my work done, but I have to plan for fun things, too. I'm always thinking about what will make my family happier. So I set up playdates and trips."

Good reads and resources

The 7 Habits of Highly Effective People: Powerful Lessons in Personal Change
by Stephen R. Covey

Organize Now!: A Week-by-Week Guide to Simplify Your Space and Your Life
by Jennifer Ford Berry and Jacqueline Musser

How To Get Organized: Plan It Then Do It
by Jill Cooper and Tawra Kellam

Organizing Solutions for People with ADHD, 2nd Edition-Revised and Updated: Tips and Tools to Help You Take Charge of Your Life
by Susan C Pinsky

Taming the To-Do List: How to Choose Your Best Work Every Day
by Glynnis Whitwer

To-Do List Makeover: A Simple Guide to Getting the Important Things Done
by S.J. Scott

Getting Things Done: The Art of Stress-Free Productivity
by David Allen and James Fallows

23. Be prepared
and do more than what is asked or expected.

Confucius said, *"Success depends upon previous preparation, and without such preparation there is sure to be failure."* Og Mandino wrote, *"Always render more and better service than is expected of you, no matter what your task may be."*

True professionals have the reputation for going above and beyond what is expected of others. The reason they are consistently able to do this is because they are better prepared. They think ahead. They do some research and gather data. They think through the options. They devote a little more time and attention to the issue, especially if it is important to the organization. When they are asked to do something by their boss or client, they can always be counted on to deliver more than what he or she expected.

What does it mean to be prepared and do more than what is asked or expected?

As a true professional, you don't show up to any meeting without having done your homework. If you are meeting people for the first time, you have looked at their profiles and know a little something about them. If the meeting is about a plan, problem, opportunity or issue, you have gathered some data and given some thought to how to proceed. You are never caught off guard by a pre-planned meeting or request. You walk into every meeting confident because you have prepared better than almost everyone in attendance. You heed the words of W. Edwards Deming: "Without data, you're just another person with an opinion."

When you are asked to do something, or to deliver something, you always exceed expectations. You give just a little bit more than what was asked or expected. People leave you thinking they got more than their money's worth. They often comment on what good value you deliver. If you are caught off guard by a surprise meeting or a last minute request which could be pivotal, you don't try to bluff your way through it unprepared. You are not afraid to say, "I wasn't expecting your call" or "I wasn't prepared for your request. Let me get back to you". You try not to leave people wanting or disappointed by a half-baked response.

A true example

My wife called me at work and asked me to pick up a few things on my way home. One of things on the list was a lottery ticket. We rarely played the lottery, but the jackpot was the largest in history. It was all over the news and everyone was talking about it. I stopped at the store, gathered the items on the list into my shopping cart, then headed over to the lottery counter. "I'm sorry," said the clerk, "but we stopped selling tickets for tonight's drawing at 7:00 pm." I was 10 minutes too late.

That evening someone won the big jackpot and my wife teased me for weeks, "Yep, that could have been us had you just gotten us a ticket." She was joking, of course, but it got me to thinking. It was the digital age. Why should I have to get in my car, drive to the store and wait in line just to purchase a $1 lotto ticket? I should be able to buy it on my cell phone and get a digital version of it, then get a text notification if I win. So began an ill fated entrepreneurial venture to build a system that enabled people to buy lotto tickets on their PC, mobile phone, or a kiosk.

I assembled a team of professionals to help design and develop the system. To create the logo and a few screen shots of the user interface I tapped Anthony, a former colleague who had created the logo and graphics for my previous company. By this time he had become very well known and was in high demand. He was also very expensive. I had a very limited budget. Anthony graciously accepted the assignment for "old time's sake". For the small amount of money I was paying him I was expecting to see one or two comps of the logo and one set of screen shots.

About a week later the team assembled for a video conference to review the work in progress. Anthony wanted to present his ideas for the logo first, because he said its look and feel would set the tone and direction for the user interface. First, he displayed the logos of every state lottery. Second, he presented the logos for the national lotto games. Third, he presented the logos of the biggest international lotto games. He discussed their similarities and differences. He explained the fonts and color schemes and what emotional responses they were designed to illicit.

Anthony then presented five different logo comps for our new system. He discussed the pros and cons of each. We were blown away; they were all amazing and it was hard to choose one. Anthony said, "Let's narrow down the top two choices, then I will run them by my user group to see if one stands out above the other." We picked the two we liked the best.

About a week later, Anthony presented the winner. He said it was favored 3 to 1 by his user group. He had also taken the liberty of stationing himself in front of the lotto counter at his local 7-11. He said it was also the favorite of the customers who had come in to buy lotto tickets. We had our logo.

Three weeks later we assembled again by video conference. Anthony was scheduled to present some screens to visualize the user interface. We all expected to view a progression of screen shots that gave a high-level overview of the menus, buttons, and navigation; more wire frame than actual design.

What Anthony presented was a completed design with high resolution graphics and fully functional menus and buttons. He started with the "home page", which looked stunning. He clicked on the various buttons and icons to display fully designed screens that went three to four pages deep. Everything worked except, of course, for the actual "programming code" which was being written by the developers. Everyone was amazed and excited to "see" how the system would be navigated and experienced by users.

Before wrapping up his presentation, almost as an after-thought, Anthony said, "Oh yeah, and I thought the marketing team could use some business cards and stationery, so I took the liberty of designing these." He flashed on the screen the collateral materials with our logo and stylized fonts. "Finally, you'll need a one-pager to convey the features and benefits of the system to partners, so here's a flyer you can either print or send as a PDF."

Anthony was a true pro in every respect. It was easy to see why he was so successful in his field. He went on to design products, applications and collateral for some of the world's largest and most iconic brands. He never charged me a penny more than the budget. He was fully enrolled in my success. He did his homework and delivered much more than was ever expected. I've sent him new clients over the years since and they always sent me a thank you note for referring him. Our lotto venture failed because of political and regulatory challenges, but Anthony's reputation continued to grow by leaps and bounds.

Data point

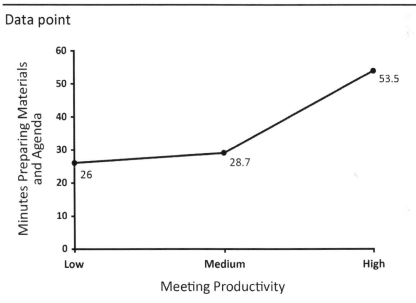

Source: A network MCI Conferencing White Paper. Meetings in America: A study of trends, costs and attitudes toward business travel, teleconferencing, and their impact on productivity.

Research proves that preparation is critical to productivity. The old saying, "Well begun is half done," is taken to heart by all true professionals. There is a direct correlation between preparation time and meeting productivity. Another old saying, "Luck is when preparation meets opportunity," is a mantra of all accomplished people. The more prepared you are, the luckier you are likely to be.

Strategies and tips for being prepared and doing more than what is asked or expected.

 So how do you put this adaptive behavior into practice?

First, never take a meeting unless you know the agenda, objectives and desired takeaways. Too many aspiring professionals walk blindly into meetings with coworkers, clients or associates without a clue as to what the meeting is about. Doing that makes you a bystander, not a valued participant. If you call the meeting, make sure you communicate the agenda, objectives and takeaways, then prepare for them accordingly. If it's someone else's meeting, insist they do the same.

Second, start with the preferred outcomes and work your way backward. Have some idea what must happen to achieve the outcomes. Know who needs to be involved and what role they need to play. Outline the high level tasks and deadlines required to achieve the desired outcomes. If you don't know what outcomes need to be achieved, at least know the questions which need to be answered to determine the best outcomes.

Third, for really important projects, conduct a dry run and try to "blow it up". You are not fully prepared unless you know what can go wrong. Most people only prepare for what can go right. A true professional also prepares for things not going according to plan. To know that, or at least have some ideas about what can go wrong, go through the entire scenario in a test environment. Perform a mock trial, test the key assumptions, or "blow up" the idea to see what can happen.

Fourth, know what is a given, what needs to be negotiated, and what can be conceded or postponed. Many pros will tell you the art of negotiation is driven by preparation. So it is true with every project and every request placed upon you. It is always easy to spot the unprepared people in the room. They get hung up on the stuff that does not matter. They debate the givens. They spend too much time talking about the trivial. The prepared professional is quick to accept the given, postpone or concede the unimportant, and make a persuasive argument for the pivotal.

Fifth, the habit of doing more than what is expected prevents you from using your reputation or relationships as a crutch. Too many aspiring professionals rest on their laurels and coast on their reputations. They are "in" with the boss and get lulled into performing at par. Even worse, some ascend to positions of power and then begin taking credit for those working under them. The biggest tip I can offer you is this: ask yourself, "What have I done that is truly laudable lately? How have I gone above and beyond what is expected of my coworkers and my peers?"

Sixth, think about everything you do in your profession in terms of value creation. You don't have to put a price on it. Remember the old saying, "Some people know the price of everything and the value of nothing." Your work may have increased the wealth of your boss or shareholders by some fixed dollar amount, but the important way to assess your contribution is by the way it helped employ people or better their lives. By thinking about ways in which you can provide superior value you will always be driven to do more than what is expected of others.

Seventh, invite your colleagues to measure you by what you do, not by what you say. Judge yourself by your actions, not by your good intentions. Durward Owen often said, "What you do speaks louder than what you say." If you adopt this as a guiding principle of your professional career, you will always push yourself to be prepared and do more than what is asked or expected.

Finally, when delivering more than expected, do it in a way that shares the credit with others. Many true professionals are better prepared and work harder than their coworkers (or perhaps even their bosses). However, they are smart enough not to make their coworkers or bosses look bad. They say things like, "Barbara gave me that idea" or "The boss inspired and challenged me to go the extra mile". Do more without alienating others and, whenever possible, present it as a team effort. This is not only a behavior of a true professional, it is a tenet of an effective leader.

The Final Word, by Ted Turner[23]

"I've never run into a guy who could win at the top level in anything today and didn't have the right attitude, didn't give it everything he had, at least while he was doing it; wasn't prepared and didn't have the whole program worked out."

Good reads and resources

The Essential Guide for Hiring & Getting Hired: Performance-based Hiring Series
by Lou Adler

Smarter Faster Better: The Secrets of Being Productive in Life and Business
by Charles Duhigg

Grit: The Power of Passion and Perseverance
by Angela Duckworth

The Most Magnificent Thing
by Ashley Spires

Exceeding Expectations: Reflections on Leadership
by William R. Looney

Exceeding Expectations: Mastering the Seven Keys to Professional Success
by Scott Weighart

Think and Grow Rich: Stickability, The Power of Perseverance
by Greg S Reid and The Napoleon Hill Foundation

Presence: Bringing Your Boldest Self to Your Biggest Challenges
by Amy Cuddy

24. Be timely, not trendy; do not chase fads or be seduced by hype.

Ralph Waldo Emerson, said, *"The art of getting rich consists not in industry, much less in saving, but in a better order, in timeliness, in being at the right spot."*

True professionals keep up with the trends, but they don't chase fads. They stay grounded. They focus on core values and principles which are sustainable over the course of their entire careers. They learn how to leverage hype, but they don't fall victim to it. They don't "drink the Kool Aid" or get distracted by the latest, shiny new things. They care more about being timely and timeless than they do about being hip and trendy.

What does it mean to be timely, not trendy; not chasing fads or being seduced by hype?

As a true professional you consider the timeliness of your major decisions and recommendations. You try not to be too early or too late. You're not afraid to place bets or take chances, but you don't do so on a whim or because everyone seems to be running in that direction. You realize how fickle and faddish some opportunities can be. You take a measured approach. You look at the fundamentals, such as the economics, growth trends, pace of technological developments, and adoption rates.

From a marketing and promotional perspective you are skeptical, but not immediately dismissive of the features and benefits promised by any opportunity. You look for validation of the promises. Red flags go up whenever anyone tells you it's a "once in a lifetime opportunity" or you "must act now or miss out". You are not afraid of walking away from anything that can't be validated or sounds too good to be true. You believe true value is gained over a period of time, not magically conjured overnight.

A true example

Chip called me out of the blue one day. I had not spoken to him since he had convinced me to invest in a startup that had since gone belly-up. "I've got a hot one!" he said. "The company is on fire. Every venture capitalist in the Valley is chasing this deal. They all want in. I'm close to the founders and invested early, so they have carved out some shares in this round for my closest friends and associates." I figured it couldn't hurt to look. "Thanks for thinking of me, Chip," I said, "Please send over the pitch deck and I'll let you know in a few days."

Chip was always chasing the new, new thing. He lived in Silicon Valley. He had invested $50,000 in a dotcom startup he made a cool $3M on. No doubt he had hit it big. He just never figured out that it wasn't because he was smarter than most of his peers, he had simply been lucky. He had been in the right place at the right time. Since making $3M a few years earlier he had plowed it all (and then some) into other high-flying tech startups. None of them had done all that well, but he had gotten the bug and was chasing every hot deal he could find.

The company he wanted me to invest in was developing artificial intelligence (AI) applications. They had a good team and a slick deck. Their projections showed them doing $100M in sales by year five. I considered the market and competitive solutions. I concluded their solution was too early. The market and the infrastructure needed to support it would not be ready for at least five years. I passed on the deal. About a year later the company was sold for "an undisclosed price". That's code for less money than had been invested. Most likely the company was acquired for the team and the shareholders got nothing.

I was an active angel investor for about 10 years. I invested in dozens of startup companies and I was a mentor for several startup accelerators. I met a lot of aspiring entrepreneurs and evaluated thousands of opportunities. My experience echoes the independent studies which have been done on startups. The single biggest reason for their failure is they are not timely. They are either way too early or a tad too late. Companies that have a so-so product and a mediocre team usually do better than companies who have a killer product and an awesome team, if their timing is better.

This phenomenon is not confined to investing in startups. The same is true for decision making in well established operating companies. Over the years I permitted my staff to adopt "leading edge" tools and processes that were all the rage of the day but turned out to deliver far less than their hype had promised. These are costly mistakes. A professional's career can be made or broken on his or her decisions and recommendations. A true professional does not get seduced by the hype of the day. He or she strives to be timely, not trendy.

Data point

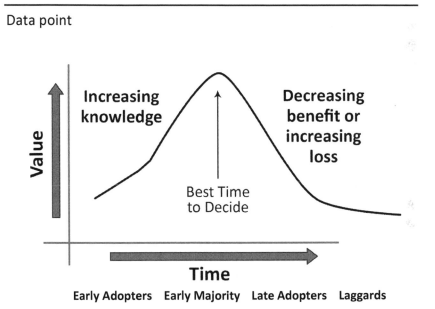

Being too late can be more deadly than being too early. Know the warning signs of analysis by paralysis. Being too comfortable with the status quo or confirmation bias – seeking information that only confirms your initial assumptions – can blind you from acting on truly good opportunities. You don't have to be an early adopter and you don't have to be a laggard. The sweet spot for most professionals is learning how to be in the early majority of the adoption curve.

Strategies and tips for being timely, not trendy; not chasing fads or being seduced by hype.

 So how do you put this internalized behavior into practice?

First, heed the saying, "Timing is everything". If you understand timing will be one of the most significant contributors to your success you won't brush it off as a cliché. Timing is good when you have good information. Timing is good when you have models and examples to build from. Timing is good when you have some control over the outcomes. Timing is good when you know more than you don't know. Timing is bad when it's based solely on hope.

Second, favor thinking and logic over passion and emotion when making big decisions or recommendations. Make the case for and against a course of action. Too many aspiring professionals let their passions and emotions get the better of them. They get seduced by the upside without thinking dispassionately about the downside. Being timely is about being balanced and weighing all possible outcomes.

Third, resist the herd instinct. Feeling like you might be "left behind" is a powerful fear that can cloud your judgment. Ask yourself some basic questions: What do they see that I don't see? What do I see that they don't see? Can these insights, either pro or con, be validated? Are people running towards it for the sake of running or do they have tangible evidence of what they will find when they get there? Do they really know how long it will take and what resources will be required or have they underestimated these things? Do we really understand the risks of taking the action or not taking the action?

Fourth, agree on how you will define success and what the metrics are along the way. What has to happen at each stage? If you are not hitting the milestones and it looks like success is much further out than you anticipated, you can slow down or rewind the decision. Being able to hit the "undo" button if the timing isn't right, or if you find out the opportunity was more hype than substance, is a critical strategy for professional success.

Fifth, be patient, to a point. The younger you are, the odds are higher you will tend to rush into things. Slow down, get grounded, make sure you are professionally and financially stable enough to give it a good go. The older you are, the less time you have to recover should an opportunity not work out, so don't get too complacent and allow truly good opportunities to pass you by (see Behavior #20).

Sixth, if you must make a quick decision and its result would not be fatal one way or the other, characterize it as "taking a flyer". Think of it like buying a lottery ticket. You're not counting on winning, but it would be a heck of a bonus if you did. If you get caught up in the hype of winning the largest jackpot in lottery history, that's fine. Not winning is not going to bankrupt you. If you decide to chase a fad your coworkers or associates want to chase, tell them you are happy to "take a flyer" but you are not going to bet your career or company on it.

Seventh, know that sustainable trends are strategic and fads are typically tactical. Strategies are long term, tactics are short term. You can make a quick buck on a fad, but they fade quickly. To build wealth you need to stick to long term trends. The same is true for your professional career. A fad gains favor quickly and has a short life. A trend gains favor slowly and has a long life. Don't be a one-hit wonder. Be a true professional by staking out a sustainable, long term strategy for your professional growth and success.

Finally, always make sure your most important professional decisions and recommendations are in alignment with your core values and principles, both as a professional or an organization. If you need to make a timely decision about your career think about how well it matches up against your professional goals. If you need to make a timely decision for your organization think about how well it matches up against the company's mission. Staying true to your core values and principles will always help you make timely decisions.

The Final Word, by Mark Cuban[24]

"In my opinion, right now there's way too much hype on the technologies and not enough attention to the real businesses behind them."

Good reads and resources

The Science of Successful Organizational Change: How Leaders Set Strategy, Change Behavior, and Create an Agile Culture
by Paul Gibbons,

Get Real: How to See Through the Hype, Spin and Lies of Modern Life
Eliane Glaser

Grounded: How Leaders Stay Rooted in an Uncertain World
by Bob Rosen

Warrior Goddess Training: Become the Woman You Are Meant to Be
by Heather Ash Amara and don Miguel Ruiz

Great Decisions, Perfect Timing: Cultivating Intuitive Intelligence
by Paul O'Brien and John Gray

Timing Is Everything: Turning Your Seasons of Success into Maximum Opportunities
by Denis Waitley

25. Be responsive, be resourceful, persevere, and finish what you start.

The noted author, Neil Gaiman, said, "*Whatever it takes to finish things, finish. You will learn more from a glorious failure than you ever will from something you never finished.*"

Accomplished people keep themselves accessible to their colleagues and associates, no matter how far up the ladder they climb. They stay responsive to the needs and inquiries of their superiors and their subordinates which prompts them to commit to what they promise and finish what they start. They don't just manage up, they manage down.

True professionals are resourceful. They don't quit easily. They develop a reputation for being closers. This harmonious duality between being responsive and finishing what they start, sticking with it, consistently earns true professionals one promotion after another and endears them to their associates.

What does it mean to be responsive, be resourceful, persevere, and finish what you start?

As a true professional you field all relevant, job related inquiries immediately. Your colleagues and associates are often surprised to receive a quick response from you, even after business hours. If you are unable to give the inquiry due attention, you acknowledge it and let the inquirer know when you will get back to him or her. Even if your response is "no thank you, not interested" you always try to provide the courtesy of a response. Your coworkers know they can always rely on you to be responsive to their questions and provide able assistance on their projects.

Upon stepping up to inquiries and projects, you can always be counted on to deliver what you say you will deliver, or that which was assigned to you. You would rather finish, knowing it is not perfect, than quit on it and make excuses for not finishing. If you honestly don't think you will be able to finish something because of other work commitments or personal circumstances, you don't accept the assignment. If such an assignment is forced upon you, you make it clear you will do your best but make no promises. It's not uncommon for you to take on more than you should, but you go the extra mile to get it all done once you commit to it. You have a reputation for resourcefulness and perseverance.

A true example

I joined CompuServe the day after my lockup was over. I had sold my second company to a publicly traded company in Seattle and was required to work for them for one year. I counted the days. The Internet revolution had dawned and I was itching to be a part of it. CompuServe was the leading online service of the time. It had just acquired a small company called Spry which had recently launched a product called "Internet-in-a-Box". The product was selling like hotcakes. Everyone wanted to get this new thing called the Internet, and Spry had it in a tidy little box. I was hired to be the Senior Product Manager to build on the momentum and rake in the dough.

Within thirty days of joining CompuServe our team quickly surmised the product was going to be in big trouble in short order. We were selling it in computer and software retail stores for $99. We were expected to triple sales in the next quarter. The problem was there wasn't anything proprietary about the product. It was comprised of a bunch of third party tools which helped people get connected to the Internet. It was essentially a marketing gimmick, not a technological marvel. Our competitors were giving away disks we were charging people for. It was clear once people and journalists figured this out our sales were going to be ZERO.

Armed with our findings and data we presented the news to the executives at CompuServe. They were stunned, especially since they had just paid a ton of money for a company that didn't own anything special and a slew of competitors were giving away the same thing we were charging for. The executives asked us what the company should do. We advised them we should throw away the Internet-in-a-Box product and become an Internet Service Provider; an ISP. This met with a lot of consternation within the executive team. It meant we would be creating a service which would compete head-to-head with CompuServe's own online proprietary service. One executive belted out, "You mean you want us to cannibalize our own product?!"

Our response was, "Customers are going to leave CompuServe in favor of an ISP anyway, so it's best to have them leave for a sister company than for a competitor." The biggest challenge was CompuServe was scheduled to go public later that year. The executives were deathly afraid the loss of revenue from Internet-in-a-Box, and an admission it was probably a rash acquisition, would negatively impact the public offering. Our small team, ably led by two senior industry executives, was undaunted. My boss stood up and said, "We will more than make up for the revenues forecasted for Internet-in-a-Box and deliver an entirely new service for CompuServe which will be loved by users and lauded by the analysts."

The CompuServe executives, in their infinite wisdom, decided to double down on the strategy. They green lighted our strategy, while also approving a separate proposal from the company's VP for building a new proprietary online service called WOW. It was designed to compete with AOL, while our new service would compete with the ISPs. The race was on. The two divisions within CompuServe became fierce competitors. We were sure that, in the end, only one new service would win.

Our small team conceived, designed, built and launched SPRYNET in just seven weeks. It was a great success. We pioneered many of the services and models still used today. It was awarded the best ISP in the country by PC Magazine and other industry publications. The WOW team spent exponentially more money, was many months late coming to market, and met with dismal reviews by customers, journalists and analysts. The WOW initiative was shut down a short time after its debut.

The SPRYNET team spent a fraction of the WOW team and went to market ahead of schedule. It accelerated CompuServe's public offering. The company went public in 1996 on the heels of SPRYNET'S successful launch and raised $500M.

This is a story about being responsive to the market and competitors, rather than denying or ignoring the inevitable. It's a story about being responsive to the company's executives, even though it required delivering them bad news. It's a story about how the team stayed responsive to each other to move mountains. It's a story about committing to a bold new plan and delivering it on time and under budget. My boss had stepped up, backed by a committed and capable team, and forever earned the golden reputation of an executive who could finish what he started with great results.

Data point

Percent of People Who Keep New Year's Resolutions

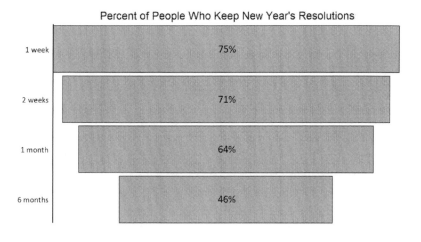

Source: Talk of the Nation, NPR

No matter what the project, research shows that many people fail to complete what they start. It's easy to quit when that's what others do and expect you will do as well. Some social scientists say this is caused by, among other things, the law of inertia and fear that the result will be less than expected. People mistakenly convince themselves it is better to not finish than to finish and be disappointed (or to disappoint others). True professionals train themselves to derive as much satisfaction from finishing, as they do from the results of what they finish.

Strategies and tips for being responsive and finishing what you start.

 So how do you put this adaptive behavior into practice?

First, have a good system for filtering out the clutter and non-productive distractions. A lot of useless stuff comes in over the transom. You need to know what is worth reading and responding to and what is not. One of the simple techniques I used in my companies was to require staff to proceed all subject lines with one of two headers: 1) Action Required or 2) FYI (For Your Information). I used the same system when sending things to clients. It's also a good practice to turn off instant notifications on your PC and phone when you need to be heads-down on a project.

Second, as covered earlier in this chapter, prioritize your work, break it into manageable parts, set deadlines, and delegate whenever possible. You should know every day what you should be working on and what can be pushed off to another day. When new inquires and requests come in, acknowledge them right away, but don't feel compelled to give them attention unless they are urgent.

Third, communicate liberally. It's almost always better to over-communicate than to under-communicate with your coworkers, clients and associates. If you are buried, let them know that and ask them not to pull you away with matters which can wait. People often don't know what you are working on or if you are on a tight deadline. They will respect your deliverables and deadlines if you ask them to do so.

Fourth, say "no" sooner rather than later. It's easy to prolong a request or carry someone along, thinking and hoping you can be responsive to them in due time. The better strategy is to say "no" right away, relaying to them you

are currently overcommitted but want to be kept on their radar for future opportunities. Saying "no" IS being responsive and your associates will respect
you for it much more than saying "maybe" and then not coming through. And
if things change and you can step up it will be a pleasant surprise and doubly
appreciated.

Fifth, for important projects and deliverables, build in cushion. If you think
it will take a week, promise it in two weeks. It's always best to under-promise
and over-deliver, then to over-promise and under-deliver. This doesn't mean
you should "sandbag" everything. Your coworkers will get wise to that strategy.
Set reasonable expectations for what needs to be done and when you can finish it.

Sixth, don't strive for perfection in everything you deliver, strive for "perfectly acceptable". Jim Collins wrote a popular book, "Good is the Enemy of
Great." This is good advice for the really, really, big things. For most things you
need to get done in your professional life you should flip this equation. Great
is the enemy of good. If you constantly struggle to make something incremen-
tally better until it is perfect, you will likely never finish it. Be content with
"good enough" for most things. The only thing that is never finished – is always
a work-in-progress – is yourself! Everything else can be and should be finished
after you commit to it.

Seventh, never commit to finish something you don't have the skills or resources to do. The iconic entrepreneur, Richard Branson said, "'If somebody
offers you an amazing opportunity but you are not sure you can do it, say yes,
then learn how to do it later!" Well, yes and no in my humble opinion. It depends upon what it is and when you are expected to do it. By all means take a
chance if you have the time to learn and perform, but it is generally ill advised
to promise to do something you do not know how to do, or don't have the
resources to finish, in the time and with the quality expected.

Finally, create the right incentives and celebrate everything you finish. Reward yourself and your team often. A professional will become what he or she
measures and rewards. The size of the reward should be commensurate with
the importance of the finished project. The everyday, completed projects, can
be celebrated with a drink after work with colleagues, or with a movie night.

The big wins can be celebrated by bonuses and vacations. Never miss an opportunity to celebrate finishing everything you started.

The Final Word, by Joyce Meyer[25]

"Getting organized in the normal routines of life and finishing little projects you've started is an important first step toward realizing larger goals. If you can't get a handle on the small things, how will you ever get it together to focus on the big things?"

Good reads and resources

The First 90 Days: Proven Strategies for Getting Up to Speed Faster and Smarter
by Michael D. Watkins

Finish What You Start
by Craig Copeland

Finish What You Start: 10 Surefire Ways to Deliver Your Projects On Time and On Budget
by Michael J Cunningham

CHAPTER 6

POLISHED

This is the ASPIRATIONAL you, how you exude confidence and <u>communicate</u> graciousness and stability.

It's about writing and speaking, how you treat others, saving and investing, doing your best and anticipating the future.

26. Communicate effectively;
write clearly and speak deliberately.

The self-help guru, Brian Tracy, wrote, "Communication is a skill that you can learn. It's like riding a bicycle or typing. If you're willing to work at it, you can rapidly improve the quality of every part of your life."

True professionals are skilled at both the written and oral word. They realize every person perceives the world differently, so they first read or listen carefully to what others are communicating then tailor their responses accordingly. It's a joy to receive an email or letter from a true pro because he or she seems to know you and understand your needs so well.

It's often inspiring to hear a true pro speak because he or she seems to echo what you are thinking and reinforce what you desire. True pros are masters at informing, entertaining, persuading, and storytelling. They can also communicate volumes with body language and facial expressions.

What does it mean to communicate effectively; write clearly and speak deliberately?

As a true professional, people don't have to figure out what you wrote or said. They quickly understand the essence of what you communicate. You have a strong command of your native language. You have a large vocabulary. You can string a proper sentence together. You don't babble on and talk for the sake of talking. Your mouth does not run faster than your brain. You think about what you need to communicate and then do so clearly, coherently, and deliberately.

In a work environment, especially when writing to customers and clients, you double check your grammar and spelling. Proofreading everything before sending is a habit. You are fully aware that how effectively you communicate can be the single most important skill for promotion. You know good communication is not about you but about who you are communicating with.

When conversing with others you are conscious of your body language and the unspoken signals you are communicating. You are also good at reading others and know instantly whether your message was received and understood by them. You pride yourself on getting to the point. After reading what you wrote or listening to what you said, your associates often comment "You nailed it!"

A true example

Midway through my term as CEO of one of the companies I started I found myself embroiled in a nasty lawsuit with a former reseller of our technology. The reseller had stolen my company's technology and was selling it to customers under their company's name. They claimed they had developed it independently, but a review of the source code proved it was ours. The lawsuit was about theft and misappropriation of intellectual property rights. I hired a well respected intellectual property (IP) lawyer to prosecute our case.

The lawsuit was expensive and protracted. It consumed much of my company's resources but we needed to win it or we would be out of business. The former reseller was with a billion dollar company. My company was a struggling startup. The opposition had three fulltime attorneys on the case. I had the one IP lawyer. It was truly David vs. Goliath.

After months of discovery and depositions we were finally ready to present a motion for summary judgment to the judge assigned to the case. My IP lawyer stood before the judge and started to plead our motion. He stuttered and stammered incoherently. He was shaking. He couldn't look at the judge or opposing counsel. He stood staring down at the papers in front of him on the lectern and literally crumbled. He simply failed to present a convincing case for the motion.

Opposing counsel presented his client's case to deny the motion and proceed to trial. He was confident and eloquent. He methodically outlined the legal arguments. He was an experienced trial lawyer. My lawyer was a brilliant IP jurist. He knew the law, he understood legal strategy, he just had no public speaking skills. In fact, I found out later, he had a terrible fear of public speaking. He should have involved another partner in his firm to help with that side of the lawsuit, but failed to do so. I knew we were going to lose the motion…and we did.

The case dragged on for more than a year. The opposition smelled blood. They could simply bury us in motions and delays and wait for us to run out of money. I was furious at my counsel's inability to communicate effectively, but I did not have the time or money to replace him. There was no chance of changing horses in midstream. My strategy was to go on the offensive and prosecute the case in the court of public opinion. I was determined to let every customer know; to inform the entire industry that our former reseller was a crook and our lawsuit was righteous. Good should prevail over unfettered corporate greed.

Opposing counsel attempted to slap a gag order on me. Rather than rely on my attorney to defend the motion in front of the judge I made the case to the judge myself. I made the point nothing I was communicating was not already in the public record and easily accessible by those in the industry. I was simply bringing it to their attention.

The judge ruled in our favor and denied the gag order motion. I blogged about the case every day. I enrolled industry leaders to come to our defense. Industry publications wrote about the lawsuit. I kept it in the news. I told the David vs. Goliath story. I made our case by appealing to the customers and influencers in the industry. I figured our adversary might beat us in court, but even if they did they would be dead in the market.

Sales of our former reseller plummeted. Customers stopped buying from them. The industry association came out publicly in our favor. The opposition was essentially beaten even if they won the case, and they knew it. They settled the case in our favor. They agreed to shut down the division selling our product and not compete in the industry for five years.

We had almost lost everything because of ineffective communication, but ended up winning because of very effective communication.

Data point

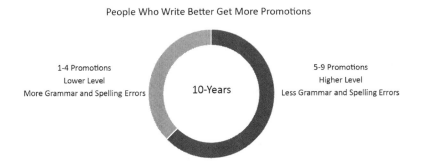

People Who Write Better Get More Promotions

1-4 Promotions
Lower Level
More Grammar and Spelling Errors

10-Years

5-9 Promotions
Higher Level
Less Grammar and Spelling Errors

Source: Grammarly

Research suggests that not only do people who write better get more promotions, the promotions they get are to higher levels than people who also get promotions, but do not write as well. Just about every survey of employers reveal that communication skills are among the most highly valued by both for-profit and non-profit organizations alike. This is especially true for professionals who supervise others.

Strategies and tips for communicating effectively; writing clearly and speaking deliberately.

 So how do you put this internalized behavior into practice?

First, read a lot. See Behavior #8. Reading a lot will help make you a better communicator. It will help you expand your vocabulary. It will subconsciously teach you good sentence structure. Reading a lot will help you become a good storyteller in your own right.

Second, write a lot. Get in the habit of blogging every week. Write a white paper for your company or industry association. Write short stories...muse about anything you fancy. Start writing a book. There are countless online forums for publishing articles. Start building a following. You will find you will write more and get better as you get feedback from people who read your works.

Third, if your work involves giving presentations, whether those presentations are for internal consumption or external consumption, take some public speaking courses. Join Toastmasters. Record videos on subjects you know, or tape product reviews and publish them online. Watch yourself. Listen to yourself. Invite others to critique your presentations.

Fourth, be a good listener. See Behavior #7. Use the other person's name in the conversation. Briefly summarize what he or she said and ask for confirmation you heard him or her correctly. This technique will give you a minute to think about how to respond in an effective manner. Train yourself to get to the point quickly. Heed the caution of George Bernard Shaw when he advised, "The single biggest problem in communication is the illusion that it has taken place."

Avoid the tendency to talk all around the point. Remember the adage: tell them what you are going to tell them; tell them; then tell them what you told them. In the words of the German artist, Hans Hofmann, "The ability to simplify means to eliminate the unnecessary so that the necessary may speak."

Fifth, be aware of non-verbal cues, both those you are sending and those you are receiving from the people you are communicating with. People need to be put at ease before they can focus on and absorb what you are saying. Smile. Make eye contact. Nod up and down slowly to let people know that, yes, you are listening. Try to avoid folding your arms and scowling; it can make others feel like you don't want to be there or care about what they are saying.

Sixth, the most effective communication is two way. If you have ever had a boss that only dictates but never takes feedback, you know how important it is to engage. The best way to start a dialogue with someone is to ask them about something they care about. After you make a point, ask them for feedback. Was it clear? Is there a better way you could have made the point?

Seventh, words matter; choose them carefully. Different words have different meanings to people. Unless slang is common among the people you are communicating with, try not to overuse it. The same goes for using buzzwords in a conversation with people who are not in your industry. Conversely, if people are throwing a lot of words at you and you are unsure of the meaning or context, don't hesitate to call them on it.

Finally, unless the topic is deadly serious, try not to take yourself too seriously when communicating with others. A good sense of humor is always appreciated. Being able to laugh at yourself is a behavior of a mature professional. There are no winners or losers in a healthy discussion. You don't have to get everyone to agree with you, or win every argument. Being understood and making a point of understanding others is what makes an effective communicator.

The Final Word, by Liz Papadopoulos[26]

"Effective communication requires more than an exchange of information. When done right, communication fosters understanding, strengthens relationships, improves teamwork and builds trust."

Good reads and resources

Looking Out, Looking In
by Ronald B. Adler and Russell F. Proctor II

Everyone Communicates, Few Connect: What the Most Effective People Do Differently
by John C. Maxwell

Crucial Conversations Tools for Talking When Stakes Are High
by Kerry Patterson and Joseph Grenny

Writing Tools: 55 Essential Strategies for Every Writer
by Roy Peter Clark

The Art of Public Speaking
by Stephen Lucas

The Definitive Book of Body Language: The Hidden Meaning Behind People's Gestures and Expressions
by Barbara Pease and Allan Pease

27. Say 'thank you' a lot; make others feel good about their efforts and contributions.

The British philosophical writer, James Allen, wrote, *"No duty is more urgent than that of returning thanks."*

You can always spot a true professional in any organization because he or she is always the one giving the credit to others. People love working with or for true professionals because they make them feel good about being there. They know how to extend a compliment and it never sounds gratuitous or disingenuous. They constantly make their coworkers and associates feel valued and appreciated. People are typically fiercely loyal to a true professional because they believe he or she will always have their backs.

What does it mean say 'thank you' a lot; make others feel good about their efforts and contributions?

As a true professional, you probably utter these two simple words more than any other: Thank you! It's a habit at work and in your personal life. You look people in the eye when you say it. They can tell you mean it. You also write a lot of thank you notes, whether they are handwritten and delivered, or typed and sent digitally. As you rise through the ranks you find frequent occasions to give people small gifts, like theater tickets, a dinner certificate, or flowers, to express your appreciation for the work they do.

You look for reasons to recognize the contributions of others. When you are introducing colleagues to your associates, you find ways to bring attention to their recent accomplishments. You tout their successes. You let them know that your own successes have been partly based on their efforts. Whenever you are receiving accolades, you are quick to share the credit. To you, almost every achievement is a team effort.

A true example

I liked Dan the moment I met him. He looked me in the eye and gave me a strong handshake. He smiled a lot when he spoke. He whispered a funny, short story, as if we had been sharing inside jokes for years. He had an air of confidence and a calm, reassuring demeanor. He was one of the most gracious human beings I had ever met.

Dan was presently "of counsel" to one of the largest law firms in town, which meant he was essentially the rainmaker. He had been an advisor to the Governors of Alaska and Oregon. An associate had introduced us after I inquired about a professional who could help me create a new entity and spin it out of the company I was working for.

Dan arranged for his law firm to incorporate my new company. He had one of his associates file a trademark on the company name and logo. He wrote the spin-out contract between my new company and the one I was working for; where I had incubated the idea. I told him I had no money; I was literally just getting started with the new venture. He smiled reassuringly and said, "No worries, I know you're good for it. A lot of the lawyers in the firm owe me a favor, so they're doing it on the QT for now. You won't get a bill for a while...maybe never." He smiled and winked.

Dan and I became fast friends and colleagues. I asked him to join the venture and he became Chairman. He lined up meetings with potential investors. He scrubbed my pitch deck and gave me presentation pointers. Right before going into any meeting he would squeeze my arm gently and whisper in my ear, "Remember, be genuine and likeable, that's more important than anything you will say."

With Dan's help the company raised $600,000 in seed money from an investor who would eventually become its biggest champion and largest investor. He also helped the company raise more than $18M from some of the best venture capital firms in Silicon Valley. I may have been the visionary and face of the company, but Dan was without a doubt the rainmaker who helped to execute on the opportunity. He was the one the investors had the most confidence in.

After the company was funded, Dan left the law firm and came aboard as fulltime Chairman. His official job was investor relations. I often kidded him his real job was making everyone feel good about being there. In less than a year we had grown to more than 100 employees. Dan knew every employee by name. We operated out of a six-story building and Dan would walk every floor, every day, talking with the employees, thanking them for their work, and making them feel good about being on the team.

Perhaps Dan's biggest contribution to the company was holding it together after an all out mutiny. I had stepped aside as CEO because the investors wanted to change to a CEO who had experience bringing companies public. The CEO they hired to replace me was truly awful. She was universally disliked by every employee. Several key employees quit. She started firing other people she feared were not loyal to her and replaced them with people who didn't like her any better. She fought constantly with the board and large shareholders who were screaming for results. She burned through $10M in less than 10 months with very little to show for it.

Throughout the whole, sad ordeal, Dan was the peacemaker between all the warring factions. He was the only one who could reason with the new CEO. He was the only one she liked and trusted. He kept the ship afloat until the investors could remove her and arrange for me to come back in as CEO and buy them out. Dan was the perfect example of grace under fire. It was one of the behaviors which made him a true professional.

Data point

Factors Employees Use to Rate Co-Workers

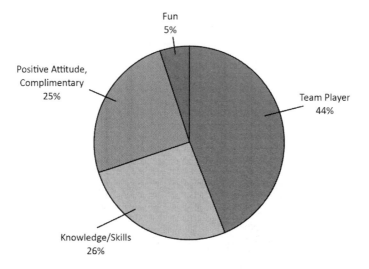

Fun
5%

Positive Attitude,
Complimentary
25%

Team Player
44%

Knowledge/Skills
26%

Source: TINYpulse Engagement Survey

Almost every workplace survey finds employees value team work and courtesy in their co-workers, more than they value their knowledge or technical skills. It's not enough to be good at what you do. You need to be good to those you do it with. 360 employee/manager reviews have become essential tools in the workforce. No longer do manager's only review their employees. Employees now review their managers and their fellow co-workers as well.

Strategies and tips for saying 'thank you' a lot, and making others feel good about their efforts and contributions

 So how do you put this internalized behavior into practice?

First, heed the adage, "People support what they help create." The reason projects fail, or worse, get sabotaged, is because people are made to feel like cogs in a wheel. People don't want to be dictated to, they want to invent and build and contribute something unique of themselves. General George Patton said, "Don't tell people how to do something. Tell them what needs to get done and let them surprise you with their ingenuity." Once people become professionally and emotionally invested in your projects and their contributions are duly recognized, there is no limit to what you can accomplish.

Second, when you must deliver bad news, do it first and get it out of the way. Then find some good news to share. Always conclude by sharing what was learned and what can be done to improve the situation. Don't hide or shy away from bad news. Deal with it head on and invite your associates to be part of the solution. If you need to reprimand someone or call them to task, always address their behaviors, their actions or lack thereof, never their opinions or them personally. And no matter how serious the issue or how vigorous you need to scold someone, always find something nice to say about them.

Third, at every opportunity, look people in the eye and give them a strong handshake. Smile when you acknowledge them. Let them know their very presence makes you feel better. In some work environments and cultures, hugs are acceptable; just make sure they are acceptable and welcomed before giving one! Remember the adage, "People won't always remember what you said, but they will always remember the way you made them feel."

Fourth, when something goes wrong between you and your colleagues or associates, ask what you did wrong or what you can do differently, even if you had nothing to do with creating the problem. You can say something like, "Could I have been more clear in my instructions?" or "Help me understand where I went wrong". Always be willing to accept at least partial responsibility for what went wrong. In most cases your colleagues will exonerate you from any miscues or wrongdoings, but they will respect you for your willingness to accept some of the blame. And of course, if you did have something to do with creating the problem own up to it immediately! Never try to deflect your own failings on others.

Fifth, be public with praise. It's always nice to whisper a word of congratulations to a coworker, but nothing beats doing it in front of others. Recognize their efforts at the weekly staff meeting. Post it on the bulletin board in the lunch room. Brag about them on social media. Some people have a difficult time promoting themselves. Be their biggest champion and promoter. They will love you for it.

Sixth, write your coworkers and colleagues a letter of recommendation. Post it on professional web sites. Do it without being asked. Always add something positive and personal about them few others know. When writing someone a letter of recommendation, never use a canned letter. Write it from the heart. Call out their skills and outstanding attributes. Let people know if your colleagues have the qualities and exhibit the behaviors outlined in this book! (Give this book a plug while you are at it ☺)

Seventh, create a funky award or recognition for your office mates or colleagues. I have seen this used effectively in all kinds of work environments. It can even be a trophy for doing something wrong, like being late for meetings or missing a deadline. The "winners" have to display it prominently on their desks until it passes to the next recipient. It's surprising what a conversation piece this can be internally and with visitors to your office.

Finally, this is going to sound a tad touchy-feely, but BE NICE and have empathy. Common courtesy is always in fashion, but too often overlooked in professional settings. People are dealing with a lot of stuff in their lives: health issues, relationship problems, debts. Be kind and considerate to everyone. You don't know what they might be going through. You might not think these are important behaviors in the work place but trust me, they are as important as any other behavior you will practice to advance your professional stature. I can't tell you how many times clients have said to me, "Mike, when it came right down to it, we decided to hire you (or your company) because you were the most LIKEABLE of the lot we had to choose from." All things being equal with your professional credentials versus someone else's credentials, you getting the nod instead of them could come down to this one behavior.

The Final Word, by Max de Pree[27]

"The first responsibility of a leader is to define reality. The last is to say thank you. In between, the leader is a servant."

Good reads and resources

Grateful Leadership: Using the Power of Acknowledgment to Engage All Your People and Achieve Superior Results
by Judith W. Umlas

A Simple Act of Gratitude: How Learning to Say Thank You Changed My Life
by John Kralik

What to Say for Compliments: 200+ Words, Phrases & Usages!
by Edit-Assist

Jane Austen's Guide to Good Manners: Compliments, Charades & Horrible Blunders
by Josephine Ross and Henrietta Webb

50 Things Every Young Gentleman Should Know Revised and Updated: What to Do, When to Do It, and Why
by John Bridges and Bryan Curtis

Be a People Person: Effective Leadership Through Effective Relationships
by John C. Maxwell

The Positive Power of Praising People
by Jerry D. Twentier

The Value-Added Employee
by Edward Cripe and Edward J. Cripe

28. Save and invest; stay disciplined, avoid shortcuts and get-rich-quick schemes.

The businessman and money advisor, Dave Ramsey, wrote, *"Financial peace isn't the acquisition of stuff. It's learning to live on less than you make, so you can give money back and have money to invest. You can't win until you do this."*

Accomplished people take the long view. They save and invest. They look for value and build wealth with discipline and patience. They don't chase the fast buck. Becoming financially independent is one of the fundamental tenants which guides their professional decisions. It gives them the ability to work for whomever they wish and walk away from any job not worthy of them. They chuckle at every get-rich-quick scheme presented to them because they know they have a better chance of being struck by lightning than they do of making a fast buck.

What does it mean to save and invest; stay disciplined, avoid shortcuts and get-rich-quick schemes?

As a true professional, you have a budget and you are good at sticking to it. You track where you spend your money. You are less concerned about acquiring things and more focused on acquiring long term wealth and financial independence. You have a savings and investment plan. Month by month you watch your debts decreasing and your positive balance increasing. You have squirreled away at least six months of living expenses in case you lose your job or are struck by unforeseen circumstances.

You watch your credit rating like a hawk. You know it can take a long time to recover from bad debts and a poor credit rating. It is often one of the things prospective employers will check before hiring you or investing in you. You realize if you are not disciplined enough to manage your own finances no company is going to want you to help manage its finances. The further you rise in your career the more responsibility you are given over the purse strings of your company and clients. You gain a reputation for managing their finances with as much diligence and care as you manage your own finances.

A true example

Like many people, Patty grew up middle class and her parents often struggled to make ends meet. Her father committed suicide when she was eight years old. Her mother had to deal with grief and guilt and mounting debts, so Patty and her sisters were shuttled between relatives. Her mother eventually remarried a man who moved the family from town to town frequently in search of odd jobs. For a short time they lived in a log cabin with no indoor plumbing and worked as ranch hands. Patty didn't have many of the modest luxuries some of her classmates took for granted. She learned the value of a dollar at an early age.

When Patty was a senior in high school a social worker told her she could qualify for some VA money to go to college because her dad had been in the military. It was only a few hundred dollars, but she jumped at the chance to make a better life for herself. She enrolled in the state university. She found a roommate and rented a small duplex. She took a full time job at a local retail store and worked her way through college. It took her five years, but the day she graduated she felt empowered to control her future.

Patty got a promotion at the retail company she worked for and transferred to a bigger city. She bought a trailer home. It was small and not much by many people's standards, but it was hers. She was a homeowner at the age of 25. Her friend from college had become a stock broker and convinced her to open an investment account. She made saving and investing a monthly habit. She had the same investment broker for 25 years and invested every spare dollar she made.

She met her husband at the retail store where she worked and had to leave her job because of the company's policy against hiring spouses. She sacrificed her career there for his career. She suffered from shyness her entire life and was deathly afraid to approach people and speak in public. She wasn't sure what to do next from a career perspective. She took a Dale Carnegie course that boosted her confidence, taught her how to express herself, and changed her life. She found a new job with NCR (National Cash Register) and was soon managing accounts like the retail giant Nordstrom.

Patty and her husband had a son. Their brokerage account grew. They invested the maximum amount every year into their son's education fund and into their IRA (individual retirement account). They bought progressively nicer homes, but rarely bought new furniture. They would either negotiate most of the furniture as part of the home purchase, or attend estate sales and buy entire room sets at a fraction of the retail cost.

Patty and her husband loved to debate which company stocks to buy. Warren Buffet was their role model. They looked for value stocks which paid dividends. They allocated a little of their portfolio to growth stocks and bought shares in a young company called Microsoft. As their wealth grew, they resisted the temptation to buy frivolous "things." When they did splurge, it was on family vacations and experiences that enriched their lives. They enjoyed life and had a lot of fun, without being reckless with their money.

They taught their son to manage his money at a very young age. He had his own stock brokerage account from the time he was 12 years old. When he went off to college they turned over to him his college fund. He had to write the checks each semester for his tuition, books and rent. He had to manage his money to make sure he made it to graduation. He had to decide what desires to sacrifice and what gratifications to delay. They told him, "Your desires must be balanced by your discipline."

Patty and her husband divorced amicably after 25 years of marriage. She went back to school and earned a Master's Degree in Acupuncture. She still spends each day managing her investments like a hawk. Her son graduated college debt free....and, wouldn't you know it, he became a wealth manager.

I am very lucky to have this amazing woman as my better half. She has been a good balance for my entrepreneurial, risk-taking outlook. Of all the behaviors required to become a true pro, this one is certainly the one I failed to practice diligently. Fortunately, I have practiced Behavior #13 and chose a domestic partner who has taught me how to live for today, but save and invest for tomorrow.

Data point

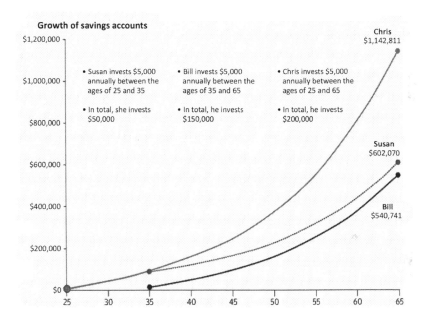

Source: JP Morgan Chase

The magic of compounded interest is well known. The addition of interest to the principal sum of a savings account is called compounding. Compound interest is interest on interest. It is the result of reinvesting interest, rather than paying it out, so that interest in the next period is then earned on the principal sum plus previously-accumulated interest.

This is how your savings account can grow exponentially over time. It is one of the most important ways in which wealth is accumulated in life. Start saving early, do it automatically with every paycheck, and never withdraw it (barring emergencies).

Strategies and tips for saving and investing; staying disciplined, avoiding shortcuts and get-rich-quick schemes

 So how do you put this internalized behavior into practice?

First, have a budget and service your debts before making any new, significant purchases. Whether it is student loans or credit card debt, getting your debts paid off as quickly as possible is the single most important step you can take. Sacrifice everything you can't absolutely live without until this is done. Heed the words of former Vice President of the United States, Joe Biden: "Don't tell me what you value, show me your budget and I'll tell you what you value." The financial thing you should value most is being debt free!

Second, if you do decide to take on financial obligations, make sure they are income producing or appreciating assets. Buy a condo or house. Invest in rental property. Make sure they are sound investments, not risky moneymaking schemes. Unless you are rolling in dough, do not buy a new car or boat. They are not only frivolous purchases; they create ongoing maintenance costs that will eat away your savings.

Third, save, save, save, with every paycheck. A habit of squirreling away a portion of all money you earn will pay huge dividends in the future. Hopefully, you understand the magic of compounded interest. Whenever your money makes money, reinvest it. Build your nest egg slowly and methodically over a long period of time. On penalty of death, do not touch it unless there is an extreme emergency.

Fourth, there are no shortcuts to financial independence. Many scammers and hucksters will try to convince you otherwise. You know the saying, "If it's too good to be true, it probably is." If someone is offering you a shortcut, you can almost always bet they will be shorting your pocketbook. This goes for investing in startup companies (something I have done a lot of unwisely). Many of the smartest, well-healed venture capitalists who do this for a living don't make money at it. Over the long haul, venture capital as an asset class does no better than the S&P (Standards and Poor) index.

Fifth, invest the maximum amount of money you can in a retirement plan every year. This allows you to reduce your taxable income. It also lets you take advantage of employer matching programs. It's free money and it grows into even more money each year. The interest is tax free when you start drawing on it at retirement. Always have a current will and medical power of attorney. No matter how modest your estate, provide for its appropriate disposition should anything happen to you.

Sixth, learn to be a good negotiator. As you go through life you will learn just about everything is negotiable. The wealthiest people you will meet are shrewd negotiators. They rarely pay full price for anything. They never overpay. They know a bargain from a bait-and-switch when they see it. They can walk away from any deal. There is nothing they can't live without if they don't get it for the right price.

Seventh, the most important investment you can make is in yourself. In the true example above, Patty invested in a Dale Carnegie course that changed her life. This isn't a onetime thing, like getting your college degree. You must continually invest in yourself – in your personal growth and professional development. A good way to invest in yourself and your future is to buy a small business, or start a company. I'm not talking about the venture-backed, swing-for-the-fences, type of company. Many people become wealthy by starting or buying a solid, profit-making small business.

Finally, never, ever, think someone is going to take care of you. Not your parents, not your kids, not your spouse, and certainly not the government. It's you against the world, no matter how big you think your inheritance is or how much your spouse loves you and promises to take care of you. Bad things happen. Life changes. The most empowered person in the world is the one who knows he or she is completely, financially, self-sufficient no matter what happens (short of the entire world economy collapsing).

The Final Word, by Suze Orman[28]

"Saving is for a short term goal that you hope to reach within five years or so. Investing is for the long term."

Good reads and resources

The Compound Effect
by Darren Hardy

The Total Money Makeover: Classic Edition: A Proven Plan for Financial Fitness
by Dave Ramsey

Saving and Investing: Financial Knowledge and Financial Literacy that Everyone Needs and Deserves to Have!
by Michael Fischer

Money Is Everything: Personal Finance for the Brave New Economy
by Amanda Reaume

Shortcuts Get You Lost: A Leadership Fable on the Dangers of the Blind Leading the Blind
by Mark Villareal

The Money Book for the Young, Fabulous & Broke
by Suze Orman

Rich Dad Poor Dad: What The Rich Teach Their Kids About Money That the Poor and Middle Class Do Not!
by Robert T. Kiyosaki

29. Do your best and face your fears; do not dwell on what you cannot control or change.

One of the authors of the New Age movement, Don Miguel Ruiz, wrote, *"Always Do Your Best. Your best is going to change from moment to moment; it will be different when you are healthy as opposed to sick. Under any circumstance, simply do your best, and you will avoid self-judgment, self-abuse and regret."*

Like all people, the most accomplished people stumble. When they do so they only get down on themselves when they know they did not do their best. And then they vow to do better the next time. The only thing they fear is their own mediocrity and complacency. They don't beat themselves up over their past failings. They don't dwell on the mistakes they made or the actions they failed to take. They learn from the past, live fully in the present, and plan for their future.

What does it mean to do your best, face your fears, and not dwell on what you cannot control or change?

As a true professional, you are not afraid of trying something new because you know you won't likely be good at it at first. In fact, you expect you might be quite bad at it but you decide to give it your best anyway. You do not fear the initial learning curve. When you do take on a new professional challenge or task you are careful to set the right expectations with yourself and your associates, then you throw yourself into it. If it's worth doing, it's worth doing right, even if the result is not perfect. You know you will get better with time and practice.

You are not one to live in the past. The past is done, it cannot be changed, but you look upon it as a teacher and guide for what you must do next. You may very well be a perfectionist, but you try not to be a control freak. You are comfortable knowing some things are simply beyond your control. You do not let that stop you from trying. If you harbor fears which are impeding your professional progress, you face them, conquer them, or at least make an uneasy peace with them that allows you to move forward. Your colleagues admire you for your "can do" spirit and because you are undaunted by change and the fear of the unknown. You heed the words of the writer, Judy Blume:

> "Each of us must confront our own fears, must come face to face with them. How we handle our fears will determine where we go with the rest of our lives. To experience adventure or to be limited by the fear of it."

A true example

After retiring as a tech entrepreneur, I took up angel investing and mentoring startups. I moved from Seattle (where I had spent most of my career) to Florida to be close to my aging parents. My mother was terminally ill; the doctors gave her about a year to live. My dad was in failing health and needed help. I did my best to help them out and started volunteering in the local entrepreneurial ecosystem, which needed a lot of assistance because it was years behind the startup ecosystems in other states.

Within a year I was offered the opportunity to run a federally funded program to start more tech companies in Florida by commercializing technologies invented at Florida universities. I almost passed on the job. I didn't know anything about university tech transfer, or working for a government agency. I was also new to Florida and didn't know the movers and shakers. How was I going to recruit all the participants, community partners, mentors, speakers, judges, board of advisors and sponsors, the job required me to do? I was still grieving the loss of my mother and helping my dad. The job would require me to move a few hours away from him. I knew I was capable, but not sure I was emotionally ready or professionally fit for this particular opportunity.

After some sleepless nights and soul searching, I decided it was the best thing I could do for myself and I accepted the job. I was determined to do the best job I could even though I was saddled with some disadvantages. I was fortunate to be paired with a partner who was well connected in the community. We worked as a team and built what became recognized as the most innovative and successful entrepreneurial training program in the state. Hundreds of aspiring entrepreneurs completed the program and several new companies were started.

On the heels of this success, I was invited to become a partner in a venture capital fund. The other partners were impressive, accomplished professionals. Although I had raised a lot of venture capital as an entrepreneur, I knew nothing about being a venture capitalist. I decided it would be a dream job and I could figure out how to be good at it. Within six months it was apparent things were not working out. Although I was getting a good handle on what it took to operate a successful venture fund, the dysfunction and poor alignment between the partners was irreconcilable.

The final straw came when I invited a dear friend and investor in my last company to visit my new venture capital firm and consider becoming a limited partner. He flew down from New York and spent the day. I introduced him to our portfolio companies and my new partners. My new partners were gracious enough to sit through a short question-answer session where my friend quizzed us on vision and strategy. When I dropped him off at the airport, my friend said, "Mike, I've got reservations about some of your partners, but I like the business model and I respect you. I'm in for $250,000." I was elated by his vote of confidence.

When I got back to the office, two of my partners were waiting for me. They were very unhappy. They admonished me for putting them in that position. One of the partners said, "That was totally off brand. We don't allow our limited partners to choose us, we choose them. They are outsourcing their judgment to us. Your friend had no right to fly down here and meet with our portfolio companies. Had we known that was going to happen we never would have permitted it."

Their arrogance and hubris were off the charts. My friend had 30 years of investment banking experience. He managed billions of dollars. Like me, none of my partners had any practical experience as venture capitalists but here they were dismissing my friend (who could run circles around them) and holding themselves out as the experts.

I resigned a short time later. I could get better at my job, but I could not control the behavior of my partners. And I was never going to risk my friend's money with partners so self-unaware as they were. A few months after I left several of the founders of the fund's portfolio companies walked out on the partners and refused to work with them. The partners had touted themselves to be the "best," without actually knowing or doing what was required to be the best.

These two stories are emblematic of doing your best, facing your fears, and not dwelling on what you cannot control or change. I did my best in both cases. I thought I might fail with the first and knock it out of the park with the second. The opposite was true. You just never know for sure. You simply do your best.

Data point

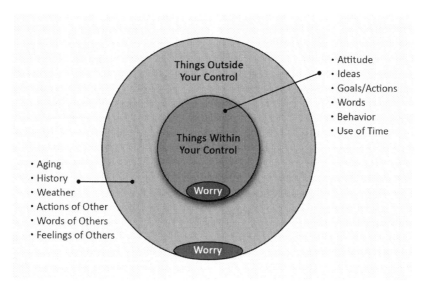

Human beings seem hardwired to worry — some more than others. Studies have found a genetic link that may make some people more prone to anxiety.

It may be one of the reasons the use of anti-depressants have skyrocketed. I am not equipped to debate the science or the medical remedies.

I can only offer this based on learning how to manage my own worries and how accomplished people have said they do so: KEEP EVERYTHING IN PERSPECTIVE. Worry a little about the things you can control, but only if you are going to do something about them. Worry very little or not at all about the things you cannot control, or are not going to take action to mitigate.

Bottom line: worry only in proportion to your willingness or ability to do something about the things that worry you.

Strategies and tips for doing your best, facing your fears, and not dwelling on what you cannot control or change.

 So how do you put this internalized behavior into practice?

First, learn to love what you cannot change about yourself. Your height, your voice, your skin and looks; your natural body size, your physical disabilities or genetic disorders. Everyone has things they wish they could change about themselves, but accomplished people learn to put their imperfections into perspective and love themselves for who they are. If others do not accept you for the things you cannot change, it is they who will never become true professionals.

Second, empathize with people's illness or misfortune, but do not let it paralyze you with fear or guilt. The best you can do for others is to stay strong and focused. The same goes for the dead and dying. Learn to grieve without allowing bits of yourself to die with them. The best way to honor the dead is to live well and remember fondly.

Third, you cannot control the weather or time. You can only make the best use of them. You cannot control your age, but you can control how you think about yourself and your life as you age. As Max Ehrmann wrote in Desiderata, "gracefully surrender the things of youth" but stay young at heart and keep fit of mind.

Fourth, you cannot control other people's opinions of you or what they say about you. What they say about you says a lot about them. If you are practicing most of the behaviors in this book, most people are saying wonderful things about you. If they are not, they are small people and of no consequence to your professional development.

Fifth, to do your best you must constantly reinvent yourself. Refuse to be labeled or stereotyped in your profession. Develop a growth mindset as opposed to a fixed mindset. Old beliefs are anchors. Do not become complacent or set in your ways. Continue to practice the timeless and universal habits that work without fail, and discard the habits that have become dated and useless.

Sixth, be quick to consider and slow to judge. Keep asking yourself, "what if?" and "can this make me better?". Get into the habit of suspending judgment, whether it be on people or opportunities. People who make snap judgments are prisoners of their own limited knowledge and experiences. They don't consider thoughtfully; they dismiss out of hand and in doing so miss opportunities to better themselves.

Seventh, before doing it, define "best". It means something different to different people. What does it mean to you in each situation? I used to compete in mini-triathlons: half mile swim, 15-mile bike, and 3-mile run. I defined "best" as finishing. I always did my best. Others define it as winning first in their age category and then train for it accordingly. You never know if you are doing your best unless you first define what best is to YOU.

Finally, almost all great discoveries and breakthroughs were achieved by accomplished people by overcoming their fear of the unknown. The outcomes of many of your important decisions in your career will be unknowable in advance. This is the one behavior that may not only distinguish you from other aspiring professionals, but the one that makes you rich and famous. If it is knowable, it may not be worth doing. Conquer the unknown and you will conquer your profession.

The final word, by Oprah Winfrey[29]

"Doing the best at this moment puts you in the best place for the next moment."

"Do the one thing you think you cannot do. Fail at it. Try again. Do better the second time. The only people who never tumble are those who never mount the high wire. This is your moment. Own it."

Good reads and resources

Mindset
by Carol Dweck, Ph.d

The Gifts of Imperfection: Let Go of Who You Think You're Supposed to Be and Embrace Who You Are
by Brene Brown

How Will You Measure Your Life?
by Clayton M. Christensen and James Allworth

StrengthsFinder 2.0
by Tom Rath

Let it Go!: Breaking Free From Fear and Anxiety
by Tony Evans

30. Anticipate the future; plan to win rather than not to lose, and accept full responsibility for your life and career.

The comedian Lewis Black quipped about life, *"When we anticipate, we're the happiest. Unless you're on antidepressants. The reason you take antidepressants is because you can't anticipate. You think everything's going to be horrible, so it usually is."*

Accomplished people are not fatalists. They firmly believe they hold their own destinies in the palms of their hands. They don't dismiss the possibility of chance or happenstance; they just believe their lives are primarily governed by the choices they make and the actions they take. They know no one is going to just hand them what they want. They don't wait for things to fall into their laps. They accept full responsibility for their lives and they don't expect to just coast through it. They want to own it.

What does it mean to anticipate the future; plan to win rather than not to lose, and accept full responsibility for your life and career?

As a true professional, you imagine the future and your starring role in it. You are always trying to control how your future will unfold. When things don't go right, or you suffer a setback, you assess your options and anticipate the tradeoffs of going in one direction versus another. You believe the harder you work the luckier you get, because you know what you are working towards.

You don't blame others or fate when you fall short. You first examine the choices you made to arrive at where you are and you are brutally honest with yourself about which choices were good and not so good. You learn from your mistakes. You own everything your life is now and will ever become. You don't always play it safe because you are not resigned to a dull and uneventful life. You hate the thought of settling for anything less than what you deserve. You have big plans and you plan to win.

A true example

There are so many rags to riches stories in our world it is impossible to highlight one over another. They are all marvelous and inspiring. Like the story I relayed about Patty (Behavior #28), I know so many people who started with nothing and built wonderfully happy, productive, and amazing lives. The vast majority of accomplished people I know are self-made. Many of them are entrepreneurs. Most professionals I know who reached the top of their fields earned the right to be there.

I subscribe to the philosophy of Jeff Bezos, the founder and CEO of Amazon.com:

> "What we need to do is always lean into the future; when the world changes around you and when it changes against you - what used to be a tail wind is now a headwind - you have to lean into that and figure out what to do because complaining isn't a strategy."

Every success story of accomplished people is unique, but they all have one common thread: they all took full responsibility for their own lives and careers. No matter what baggage or challenges they were saddled with, they dealt with them and moved on. They never played the victim. They refused to wallow in self pity.

I want this example to be **YOUR story**. I hope you will write me one day and tell it. With that, I give you my two, all-time favorite quotes. The first from Theodore Roosevelt:

> "It is not the critic who counts; not the man who points out how the strong man stumbles, or where the doer of deeds could have done them better. The credit belongs to the man who is actually in the arena, whose face is marred by dust and sweat and blood; who strives valiantly; who errs, who comes short again and again, because there is no effort without error and shortcoming; but who does actually strive to do the deeds; who knows great enthusiasms, the great devotions; who spends himself in a worthy cause; who at the best knows in the end the triumph of high achievement, and who at the worst, if he fails, at least fails while daring greatly, so that his place shall never be with those cold and timid souls who neither know victory nor defeat."

And the second from Hunter Thompson:

> "Life should not be a journey to the grave with the intention of arriving safely in a pretty and well preserved body, but rather to skid in broadside in a cloud of smoke, thoroughly used up, totally worn out, and loudly proclaiming "Wow! What a Ride!"

It's your life and your future. Own every minute of it!

Data point

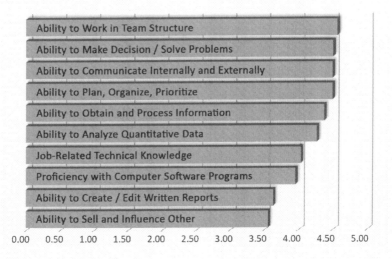

Weight of Skill / Quality on 1-5 Scale

Source: National Association of Colleges and Employers

One of the ways to be successful in the future is to know what the future will need. From a professional qualities perspective, consider the chart above. The future requires team-work, problem-solving, decision-making, planning and organization. That's pretty much what the future has always required – thus the importance of the universal and timeless qualities championed herein. No matter what your profession, these qualities will vastly increase your chances of future success.

Strategies and tips for anticipating the future; planning to win rather than not to lose, and accepting full responsibility for your life and career.

 So how do you put this adaptive behavior into practice?

First, have a plan for your life and for your career. People who say they don't need a plan actually have one: it's a plan not to plan and accept whatever happens. There are many sports and military analogies on this subject. If you have played sports or served in the military you already know the team that wins is the one which wants it more and works the hardest. A good plan has goals and objectives. It has strategies and tactics. It's adjusted frequently as needed, based on real world feedback and results. The professionals who win big are not always the ones with the best plan. They are the ones who never quit planning.

Second, always have a current resume. Keep your online professional profile up to date. Don't ever look stale or dated. Have a current picture. List your positions, volunteer activities, and achievements. Post and share articles. Your professional connections should think to themselves: "This is an impressive person who is always growing, always moving forward, and always becoming a better version of himself or herself."

Third, understand the past and use it to connect the dots in the future. People who anticipate and connect the dots are the ones who invent the future. Steve Jobs was a genius at doing this. In a commencement address to Stanford, he said:

> "You can't connect the dots looking forward; you can only connect them looking backwards. So you have to trust that the dots will somehow connect in your future. You have to trust in something – your gut, destiny, life, karma, whatever. Because believing that the dots will connect down the road will give you the confidence to follow your heart even when it leads you off the well-worn path; and that will make all the difference."

Fourth, read about the future. It's almost scary how the scientific breakthroughs and technical gadgets predicted by futurists and sci-fi writers have some to pass. When I was just starting my career, I read Alvin Toffler's "Future Shock" and John Naisbitt's "MegaTrends." These books had a profound impact on me. They led me to choose computers, software and subsequently the Internet as my career path. Before reading them I was planning to become a lawyer. In hindsight, it was a great choice. I'll be really excited when we get the holodeck!

Fifth, I know it's a cliché', but gravitate to something you are passionate about AND leverages your talents and skills. Imagine the future 50 years from now. What does the world look like? Have we colonized other planets? Are we living below the oceans? How is everything powered? How are we doing it without destroying the planet? How many more people will there be and how are we feeding them? Will there be countries and borders? How are people getting around? What will be obsolete by then? What will the world need most when you are 60 years old? What role do you want to play in all that?

Sixth, visualize yourself being successful. Visualization is a powerful, often underrated technique. Visualize what you will be doing 10 years from now. Will you be running your own company? Traveling the world? What contributions will you be making? How will you be teaching and inspiring others? Write your future self a letter with your goals and plans; your hopes and aspirations. Re-read it every year when you sit down to plan your annual goals.

Seventh, prepare yourself for sudden misfortune, but do not allow the possibility of failure or setback to make you too cautious. I know people who made and lost millions of dollars several times in their lives. They never got too comfortable when they were on top and they never got too scared when they hit bottom. They never stopped believing in themselves because they continually worked to acquire the qualities and practice the behaviors outlined in this book.

Finally, it may sound selfish, but you must absolutely, positively, live for yourself. You have to give yourself permission to live the life you want. You cannot live solely for others; not your parents, not your kids, and not your spouse. You will be able to do more for others once you have learned to live for yourself. Others might attempt to guilt you into living for them or their institutions. They might attempt to brainwash you into thinking sacrifice and dedication to their beliefs and ideals, at the expense of your own needs and wants, is the righteous path of a good person. You can best serve those you love and the greater good by staying true to yourself and living the life you want.

The Final Word, by Michael Korda[30]

"Success on any major scale requires you to accept responsibility. In the final analysis, the only quality that all successful people have is the ability to take on responsibility."

Good reads and resources

The Future: Six Drivers of Global Change
by Al Gore

The Industries of the Future
by Alec Ross

Elon Musk: Tesla, SpaceX, and the Quest for a Fantastic Future
by Ashlee Vance

HBR's 10 Must Reads Boxed Set (6 Books) (HBR's 10 Must Reads)
by Harvard Business Review and Peter Ferdinand Drucker

The Future of the Professions: How Technology Will Transform the Work of Human Experts
by Richard Susskind and Daniel Susskind

Playing to Win: How Strategy Really Works
by A.G. Lafley and Roger L. Martin

Accepting Responsibility for Oneself
by Gloria J. Edmunds Ph.D.

Stepping Up: How Taking Responsibility Changes Everything
by John B Izzo and Marshall Goldsmith

DURWARD W. OWEN, BIOGRAPHY

 Durward W. Owen, Certified Association Executive (CAE), served as the Executive Director of Pi Kappa Phi, a national collegiate fraternal organization, from July 1959 until August 1994. Under his tenure, the organization grew 171% from 52 chapters nationwide to 141 chapters including 11 associate chapters. Membership grew 368%, from 18,925 members to 69,624 members, and the financial assets of the organization grew by more than 3,000%.

Mr. Owen's career was devoted largely to pioneering and implementing social, educational and leadership programs for young people with an emphasis on experiential learning. His mantra for the organization he led for 35-years was "...a very personal fraternity...a very personal experience." As noted in this book, he emphasized the importance of professionalism and taught thousands of young people the core qualities he observed in successful people across all professions.

Mr. Owen founded Pi Kappa Phi Properties, Inc., which has owned and operated over the years since its inception in 1966 more than 34 student living facilities on college campuses. He also founded Push America (later renamed the Ability Experience), a national 501 c3 philanthropy to recognize, value and support people with disabilities. The Ability Experience has raised millions of dollars and donated millions of man hours to increase acceptance and understanding of disabled people in the workplace while developing young people into servant leaders.

Mr. Owen is the Past President of the Fraternity Executive Association, the College Fraternity Editors Association, and the Western Carolina Center Foundation. He served on North Carolina Governor's Advocacy Council for Children and Youth, on the board of the North Carolina School of the Arts Foundation, and was a long-time member of the American Society of Association Executives. He has received numerous national honors and awards for distinguished service and extraordinary contributions to his profession.

Of special note is the contribution Mr. Owen made to the entire college Greek system by founding the Fraternity Insurance Purchasing Group (FIPG), an organization which provides risk management programming and education to collegiate fraternal and sorority organizations. At a time of skyrocketing insurance costs which threatened the very existence of many collegiate fraternal organizations, Mr. Owen also mobilized the industry into unprecedented cooperation to self-insure itself through the formation of a fully-funded captive insurance company, FRMT, Ltd. Many in the collegiate fraternal world believe Mr. Owen's efforts helped save the Greek system from major financial problems, by defending and reducing liability costs.

Mr. Owen served in both the Army and Airforce. He received his Bachelor of Arts Degree from Roanoke College and his Master of Business Administration Degree from Florida Atlantic University. He and his wife of 64-years, Connie, raised three children and live in Charlotte, North Carolina. He is retired, but still active in various charitable and community organizations.

ABOUT THE AUTHOR

Michael O'Donnell, author, entrepreneur, and mentor to many, has worn numerous hats over his long career. He has been a serial entrepreneur, venture capitalist, angel investor, mergers and acquisitions professional, and trusted coach and confidant to aspiring and seasoned entrepreneurs alike. He is the author of several best-selling books on business planning and marketing planning, and is a popular blogger and speaker on all things startup. His latest passion is championing the principles of professionalism with the Millennial generation.

Mike O'Donnell started his high-tech career in 1983 as a co-founder of one of the first high-speed electronic publishing service bureaus in the United States. In 1985, he founded Ask Me Multimedia Systems, where he served as its president and CEO for 10 years. Under his leadership, Ask Me Multimedia pioneered some of the first multimedia kiosks, authoring software and presentation programs. In 1991, Ask Me Multimedia received the prestigious National Small Business Innovation Award from Nations Business Magazine and the U.S. Chamber of Commerce.

After selling Ask Me Multimedia in 1995, Mike embraced the Internet revolution and joined CompuServe as a key executive. While at CompuServe, he helped lead the launch of SPRYNET, one of the nation's first Internet Service Providers (ISP), which went public in 1996. PC Magazine named SPRYNET as the best Internet Service Provider in the nation.

In 1997, while serving as Director of Electronic Commerce for Design Intelligence (later acquired by Microsoft), O'Donnell conceived, built and launched the Internet's first automated digital content licensing system, called iCopyright.com. He raised more than $30M in venture capital, negotiated global contracts with many of the world's leading publishers, and led the company for more than 10 years, before stepping aside to pursue other entrepreneurial interests. iCopyright was named one of the Top 100 Companies That Matter Most in the Digital

Content Industry five years in a row by eContent Magazine, and received the prestigious SIIA CODiE award three times, the industry's highest honor for technical excellence and innovation.

Between 2010 and the present, Mike led several startup accelerators, launched a venture capital firm, and invested in dozens of startup companies as an angel investor. In 2016, Mike joined a business brokerage firm to specialize in mergers and acquisitions of tech-related companies. In his spare time, he writes and speaks on the role professionalism plays in accelerating career and life success.

Mike attended the University of Florida and completed the Executive Management Program at Stanford University. He is the father of three children, who continue to be his biggest achievement and source of pride. He lives in Fort Lauderdale, Florida, with the love of his life, Patty, and their adorable Maltese Poodle, Moxie.

You can connect with Mike on Linkedin at:
https://www.linkedin.com/in/mikeodonnell

ONLINE RESOURCES

For more information on the people quoted herein, the books recommended herein, and for access to additional interactive resources on professional development and career advancement, please visit *aTruePro.com*.

Notes

[1] Daymond John is an American entrepreneur, investor, television personality, author and motivational speaker. He is best known as the founder, president, and CEO of FUBU, and appears as an investor on the ABC reality television series Shark Tank.

[2] Jacqueline Whitmore is an etiquette expert, author and certified speaking professional. She is also the founder of The Protocol School of Palm Beach, a premier business etiquette consulting firm dedicated to helping executives polish their professionalism, enhance their interpersonal skills, and improve their personal brand.

[3] Kayla Itsines is a fitness guru, author and motivational speaker. Her example and inspiring posts have attracted more than 10M followers.

[4] Dr. Phil McGraw is is an American television personality, author, psychologist, and the host of the television show Dr. Phil. Forbes ranked him the 15th highest earning celebrity in the world.

[5] Dan Harris is a correspondent for ABC News, an anchor for Nightline and co-anchor for the weekend edition of Good Morning America. He is also the author of *10% Happier: How I Tamed the Voice in My Head, Reduced Stress Without Losing My Edge, and Found Self-Help That Really Works — a True Story*.

[6] Fareed Zakaria is an Indian American journalist and author. He is the host of CNN's Fareed Zakaria GPS and writes a weekly column for The Washington Post. He has been a columnist for Newsweek, editor of Newsweek International, and an editor-at-large of Time. He is the author of five books, three of them international bestsellers.

[7] Roy T. Bennett is the author of The Light in the Heart. He loves sharing positive thoughts and creative insight that has helped countless people to live a successful and fulfilling life.

[8] Fran Lebowitz is an American author and public speaker. She is known for her sardonic social commentary on American life as filtered through her New York City sensibilities. Some reviewers have called her a modern-day Dorothy Parker.

[9] Theodore Rubin is an American psychiatrist and author. He is a past president of the American Institute for Psychoanalysis and the Karen Horney Institute for Psychoanalysis. He is a long-time contributing columnist to the Ladies' Home Journal and the author of more than twenty-five works of fiction and nonfiction.

¹⁰ Malala Yousafzai is a Pakistani activist for female education and the youngest-ever Nobel Prize laureate. She is known mainly for human rights advocacy for education and for women in her native Swat Valley in the Khyber Pakhtunkhwa province of northwest Pakistan, where the local Taliban had at times banned girls from attending school. Yousafzai's advocacy has since grown into an international movement.

[11] Kate White is an American writer, magazine editor, and speaker. From 1998 to 2012, she served as the editor-in-chief of Cosmopolitan.

[12] Gretchen Rubin is an American author, blogger and speaker. She received her undergraduate and law degrees from Yale University, was editor-in-chief of the Yale Law Journal and won the Edgar M. Cullen Prize. She clerked on the U.S. Supreme Court for Justice Sandra Day O'Connor and served as a chief adviser to Federal Communications Commission Chairman Reed Hundt.

[13] Ashton Kutcher is an American actor and investor. He began his career as a model and began his acting career portraying Michael Kelso in the Fox sitcom That '70s Show, which aired for eight seasons. He made his film debut in the romantic comedy Coming Soon and became known by audiences in the comedy film Dude, Where's My Car?, which was a box office hit. He created, produced, and hosted Punk'd which aired on MTV for five seasons until its revival in 2012.

[14] Colin Powell is an American statesman and a retired four-star general in the United States Army. He was the 65th United States Secretary of State, serving under U.S. President George W. Bush from 2001 to 2005, the first African American to serve in that position. During his military career, Powell also served as National Security Advisor (1987–1989), as Commander of the U.S. Army Forces Command (1989) and as Chairman of the Joint Chiefs of Staff.

[15] Ann Voskamp is the author of the New York Times Bestseller, One Thousand Gifts: A Dare to Live Fully Right Where You Are. Named one of Publishers Weekly's Bestsellers for the year of 2011 and a USA Today Bestseller, Voskamp's debut memoir received an award of merit in Christianity Today's Books of the Year in 2012 while her blog was named in the Top 100 blogs of 2011 by Babble.

[16] Werner Erhard is an American critical thinker and author of transformational models and applications for individuals, groups, and organizations. He has written about integrity, performance, leadership and transformation

[17] Lao Tzu was an ancient Chinese philosopher and writer. He is known as the reputed author of the Tao Te Ching and the founder of philosophical Taoism, and as a deity in religious Taoism and traditional Chinese religions

[18] James A. Owen is an American comic book illustrator, publisher and writer. He is known for his creator-owned comic book series Starchild and as the author of The Chronicles of the Imaginarium Geographica novel series, that began with Here, There Be Dragons in 2006.

[19] Dolly Parton is an American singer-songwriter, multi-instrumentalist, actress, author, businesswoman, and humanitarian, known primarily for her work in country music. She is the most honored female country performer of all time.

[20] Vanessa Hudgens is an American actress and singer. She rose to prominence playing Gabriella Montez in the High School Musical series. She has also appeared in various films and television series for the Disney Channel.

[21] Anthony Robbins is an American businessman, author, motivational speaker and philanthropist. He became well known from his infomercials and self-help books: Unlimited Power, Unleash the Power Within and Awaken the Giant Within.

[22] Heidi Klum is a German-American model, television personality, businesswoman, fashion designer, television producer, and occasional actress

[23] Ted Turner is an American media mogul and philanthropist. As a businessman, he is known as founder of the Cable News Network, the first 24-hour cable news channel.

[24] Mark Cuban is an American businessman and investor. He is the owner of the National Basketball Association's Dallas Mavericks, Landmark Theatres, and Magnolia Pictures, and is the chairman of the HDTV cable network AXS TV and appears as an investor on the ABC reality television series Shark Tank.

[25] Joyce Meyer is a Charismatic Christian author and speaker and president of Joyce Meyer Ministries. Meyer and her husband Dave have four grown children, and live outside St. Louis, Missouri.

[26] Liz Papadopoulos is the Chair of the Ontario College of Teachers and an educator in professional communications.

[27] Max de Pree is an American businessman and writer. His book *Leadership is an Art* has sold more than 800,000 copies. In 1992, De Pree was inducted into Junior Achievement's U.S. Business Hall of Fame.

[28] Suze Orman is an American author, financial advisor, motivational speaker, and television host. She was born in Chicago and pursued a degree in social work. She worked as a financial advisor for Merrill Lynch.

[29] Oprah Winfrey is an American media proprietor, talk show host, actress, producer, and philanthropist.

[30] Michael Korda is an English-born writer and novelist who was editor-in-chief of Simon & Schuster in New York City.

Made in the USA
Charleston, SC
06 January 2017